UNIVERSITY OF NORTH CAROLINA AT CHAPEL HILL
DEPARTMENT OF ROMANCE LANGUAGES

NORTH CAROLINA STUDIES
IN THE ROMANCE LANGUAGES AND LITERATURES

Founder: URBAN TIGNER HOLMES

Distributed by:

UNIVERSITY OF NORTH CAROLINA PRESS
CHAPEL HILL
North Carolina 27514
U.S.A.

NORTH CAROLINA STUDIES IN THE
ROMANCE LANGUAGES AND LITERATURES
Number 194

MONTAIGNE AND FEMINISM

MONTAIGNE AND FEMINISM

BY
CECILE INSDORF

CHAPEL HILL

NORTH CAROLINA STUDIES IN THE ROMANCE
LANGUAGES AND LITERATURES
U.N.C. DEPARTMENT OF ROMANCE LANGUAGES
1977

Library of Congress Cataloging in Publication Data

Insdorf, Cecile.
  Montaigne and feminism.
  (North Carolina studies in the Romance languages and literatures; no. 194)
  Bibliography: p.

  1. Montaigne, Michel Eyquem de, 1533-1592—Relationship with women.
  2. Feminism—History. I. Title. II. Series.
PQ1645.I5   844'.3   77-24733
ISBN 0-8078-9194-0

I. S. B. N. 0-8078-9194-0

DEPÓSITO LEGAL: V. 2.465 - 1977   I.S.B.N. 84-399-7340-3
ARTES GRÁFICAS SOLER, S. A. - JÁVEA, 28 - VALENCIA (8) - 1977

ACKNOWLEDGEMENTS

   I would like to take this opportunity to record my gratitude to Professor Henry Hornik for his guidance and wise advice over several years. To a great extent, these pages are the result of his patience and encouragement.
   To Professor Alex Szogyi I express my appreciation for his careful reading, criticism and intelligent comments.
   A special words of thanks is due to Professor Henri Peyre who suggested that I write this study. His kind assistance and helpful suggestions proved invaluable.
   I owe a tremendous debt to Annette for her skills as both typist and daughter, and above all, to my husband Michael for his understanding and unselfish support.

TABLE OF CONTENTS

	Page
Acknowledgements	7
Introduction	11

Chapter

I.	The Role of Women in Society Prior to the Sixteenth Century	13
II.	The Role of Women During the French Renaissance	20
	"La Querelle des femmes"	24
III.	Influences of Antiquity	31
IV.	Montaigne's Personal Background and Women	41
	Montaigne's Appearance	41
	Montaigne and His Mother	43
	Montaigne and His Wife	47
V.	Montaigne and Marie de Gournay	59
	Her Role in the History of Feminism	59
	Her Influence on Montaigne	64
VI.	Montaigne's Concepts of Womanhood	72
Conclusion		92
Bibliography		96

INTRODUCTION

Perhaps some readers will be surprised by this title, surprised by the possibility that Montaigne could be discussed within the context of feminism. Although Montaigne has been depicted as rather antifeminist in some critical works, the purpose of this study is to expose his other views in this area and to consider his possible duality with regard to women.

My main interest is not to prove Montaigne a feminist; perhaps enough antifeminism characterizes his writings to disqualify him from such an absolute category. However, I consider it a tribute to his all-encompassing mind that many profoundly feminist considerations also find a place in his *Essais*. Montaigne's relationships were of such a complex and contradictory nature that we must examine his two sides, one of which may be termed feminist.

Rather than simply apply a twentieth-century feminist sensibility to this Renaissance author, I would like to suggest that part of Montaigne's enduring quality may lie in his paradoxical treatment of timeless feminist questions. Of course, to understand the dichotomy in Montaigne's relationships with women not only gives us a greater appreciation of the essayist but places feminism in a long perspective.

Although Montaigne was not directly involved in the famous "Querelle des femmes" of the sixteenth century, the arguments were in the air and could not help but filter into his writings. It, therefore, becomes essential to examine some of the theories which were prevalent at the time; I believe his concepts of womanhood can be viewed only within the framework of his society.

CHAPTER I

THE ROLE OF WOMEN IN SOCIETY PRIOR TO THE SIXTEENTH CENTURY

Feminism became an important movement in France during the Renaissance; however, the question of women's role in society had already been the cause of a "querelle" in the previous century. In order to place feminism in a proper historical context, we must therefore return to the Middle Ages.

We already find in the Middle Ages numerous attacks on "the weaker sex," and it is obvious that degradation of women is much more the mode than praise. In fact, criticism of women is one of the most characteristic traits of medieval literature. The Bible was the most important reference of the time, unquestionably declaring the inferior position of the woman. As Maurice Valency puts it, "the head of every man is Christ and the head of the woman is the man. All the weight of church was massed behind this doctrine." [1] In their eagerness to exalt the spiritual ideal of chastity, certain theologians accused women of great vices. According to them, "women were believed to be naturally inclined to virtually boundless lust." [2] This view is evidently rooted in the conception of Eve and subsequent associations of the woman with the temptress or original sinner. As Simone de Beauvoir elucidates, "in a religion that holds the flesh accursed, woman becomes the devil's most fearful temptation." [3]

---

[1] Maurice Valency, *In Praise of Love: An Introduction to the Love Poetry of the Renaissance* (New York, 1958), pp. 62-63.

[2] M. A. Screech, *The Rabelaisian Marriage* (London, 1958), p. 6.

[3] Simone de Beauvoir, *The Second Sex*, trans. H. M. Parshley (New York, 1953), p. 97.

In *Women in Antiquity*, Charles Seltmann delves into the intimate relationship between religion and anti-feminism during the Middle Ages. He finds that "the defamation of half — the female half — of humanity ... led, through a fear of woman and sex, to a terrible escape into vowed celibacy and chastity." [4] Theologians developed a world view of the female sex that may be considered as nothing less than monstrous. From this view arose a general hostility towards women.

The problem of the love of God enflamed the theologians of the twelfth and thirteenth centuries and did not end with them; according to Emile Telle, polite society at the end of the twelfth century, notably the court of Marie de Champagne, took an avid interest in this problem and sought to transfer the theological discussions of divine love to their secular level. "Les clercs se chargeaient alors d'élaborer une religion éthérée de l'amour humain à l'instar des aspirations sacrées des théologiens." [5]

Seltmann, however, puts this in a different light: "From the religiously induced horror of sex and woman mankind must find an escape, and ... it was found in the cult of the Virgin Mary." [6] The psychological roots of this religious cult extend into secular cults; woman is most easily dealt with when polarized into either Eve or Mary:

> ... for the fear and hatred of Eve, and of what she represented through the persons of girls and women, having become an obsession of male celibates, it was inevitable that relief must be found in the concept of a Mothergoddess. Naturally the medieval Church was united to a patriarchal system wherein women were servants and dependents of men. Yet docile service and unquestioning obedience could redeem them, and these qualities were thought to exist in the Mother of Christ, handmaid of the Lord — who was at the opposite pole from Eve the sinner — Mary, who was the mediatrix of salvation, and therefore an offset to Eve, the mediatrix of damnation. [7]

---

[4] Charles Seltmann, *Women in Antiquity* (New York, St. Martin's Press, n.d.), pp. 202-203.

[5] Emile V. Telle, *L'Œuvre de Marguerite d'Angoulême, reine de Navarre et la querelle des femmes* (Toulouse, 1937), p. 13.

[6] Seltmann, p. 204.

[7] *Ibid.*, p. 205.

Christian thought was secularized in favor of the woman who became the object of the cult "Domina." But this unattainable ideal could not help but provoke a highly negative reaction to the actual woman of the time. The ideal of "Love" was in sharp opposition to the trivialities of conjugal life.

The medieval wife was simply the husband's property, a child-bearing, house-tending necessity, devoid of romantic appeal. She was not even an object of sexual pleasure. Maurice Valency tells us, "the ideal compromise between concupiscence and abstinence would thus be found in cohabitation for utility and not for pleasure, and this doctrine effectively excluded passion from the good marriage." [8]

The embodiment of the conflict between the ideal woman and the real woman in literary forms (which occurred in the second half of the twelfth century) served only to intensity this dichotomy. According to Telle, "l'axiome de l'amour courtois qui déclare que l'amour et le mariage sont incompatibles entraînait la critique du mariage au nom de cet amour. Ceci créa entre 1150 et 1200 environ une littérature galante et courtoise toute d'imagination qui débordait le monde raffiné et initié à qui elle était destinée pour s'étendre au public bourgeois." [9] Marriage was therefore attacked in both the name of spiritual love and the evils of conjugal life. We need only be aware of the disparity between the exalted lady and the poor housewife to comprehend the latter's pitiful position.

This condemnation of marriage brought about a curious reaction in the form of the pure love of the chevalier on the one hand and common infidelity on the other. With the advent of courtly love, every respectable lady had a Platonic 'serviteur' as well as an ordinary husband. The other side of this coin is well expressed by C. S. Lewis: "Any idealization of sexual love, in a society where marriage is purely utilitarian, must begin by being an idealization of adultery." [10] And, moreover, the fabliaux and farces lead us to believe that unfaithfulness was quite common.

The initial point of the "Querelle" against and subsequently for women was, therefore, the conflict between love and marriage. Courtly society and its literature transposed this question from the

---

[8] Valency, p. 19.
[9] Telle, p. 13.
[10] C. S. Lewis, *The Allegory of Love* (London, 1936), p. 13.

Christian domain to the secular "pour faire du chevalier le parfait amant. L'amour du chevalier pour la Dame est devenu la copie de celui du chrétien pour son Dieu." [11] This phenomenon would also have its cult and its dogmas, as formulated by the *Arts d'Amour*, among which the best known is that of André le Chapelain.

According to this theory, the lover found himself in an inferior position with regard to the lady. It was necessary to follow the courtly code scrupulously, love being an art, even a science, which posited its rules. These rules had to be obeyed, at the risk of being judged unworthy. Jean Frappier tells us that "l'amour courtois est en principe un amour de loin, fortifié par l'absence et par les obstacles." [12] And if we consult the major literary works of this era, we find the manifestation of this intellectual conception of love, as well as the more concrete poems of amorous intent.

Alain Chartier's *La Belle dame sans mercy* focuses on the suffering of the unsuccessful lover, but his object is less an idealization than a tangible woman. Rather than being an art, love is a frustrating attempt to win the woman's favors, a dramatic dialogue in which both parties give voice to their emotions. The poem opens with typical courtly images: women are "juges" who hold men as prisoners, "en leurs lyens." [13] But it moves through a series of arguments in which the Amant tries to overcome the fears of the Belle Dame. There is a psychological sophistication in her responses that seems to go beyond courtly convention; her last words make the lover responsible for his situation, unable to shift the blame to herself or to Fortune: "Riens ne vous nuit fors vous meismes. / De vous mesmes juge soyez." [14] By contrast, the novels of the Round Table and the songs of the troubadours reveal the more idealized attitude of the time.

A serious problem arises when the very clergymen who had helped create these theories of courtly love were now judged unfit to love. So they, in turn, renewed their attacks on marriage and women by showing how man is reduced by the spiritual and material servitude of conjugal life. This repeated condemnation gave rise

---

[11] Telle, p. 14.
[12] Jean Frappier, *La Poésie lyrique en France au XIIe et XIIIe siècles* (Paris, 1962), p. 94.
[13] Alain Chartier, *La Belle dame sans mercy* (Paris, 1945), p. 5.
[14] *Ibid.*, p. 32.

to a hostility which transcended the literary domain and had a primary impact on the attitude of the male sex.

In the formation of this attitude, the courtly love convention is, therefore, of great importance; we cannot ignore the difference between the theoretical adoration of the woman and the common practice, between the "amour courtois" and the manner in which she was treated by her contemporaries. At the same time, we should be aware that a single phenomenon known as courtly love may never have existed at all. Moshé Lazar in his illuminating study, *Amour Courtois et "Fin'Amors" dans la littérature du XIIe siècle,* is careful to distinguish among three distinct aspects of the courtly attitude: courtoisie, fin'amors and amour courtois. And even within the category of "amour courtois," there are significant shades of difference: "Si l'amour courtois est un art d'aimer, une certaine manière de vivre et de chanter l'expérience amoureuse, il n'est pas le même pour les poètes du Midi, pour Marie de France ou pour Chrétien de Troyes." [15] Rather than viewing these songs of love as disembodied replicas of religious adoration, Lazar claims that they are sensual in origin — especially fin'amors — derived in opposition to the Church. [16] The physical realities of fin'amors cannot be ignored: "Elle a pour objet à la fois le cœur et le corps de la femme mariée." [17]

The implications of Lazar's analysis should be noted. While his interpretation grants the woman more of a physical reality than other critics', the emphasis falls perhaps too heavily on the carnal aspect. Lazar makes it clear that her body is the source and end for the lover, beauty being the main force:

> C'est, au contraire, une chaude sensualité, une morale vouée au plaisir des sens, que nous avons découvertes à la base de la fin'amors. La spiritualité et l'éthique chrétiennes n'y tenaient nulle place. [18]

---

[15] Moshé Lazar, *Amour Courtois et "Fin'Amors" dans la littérature du XIIe siècle* (Paris, 1964), p. 23.
[16] *Ibid.,* p. 12.
[17] *Ibid.,* p. 61.
[18] *Ibid.,* p. 103.

Depending on the interpretation, therefore, the courtly love phenomenon offers us the polarities of woman as abstraction or woman as body.

The most noteworthy and influential document of the period in this context is the *Roman de la Rose,* a work whose popularity lasted more than three centuries. Its subject is the art of love (the book was simultaneously an allegorical story of a romantic conquest and a treatise on love). The first part, by Guillaume de Lorris, represents the courtly ideal, and he announces at the outset that he wishes to give his public a work "ou l'art d'Amors est toute enclose." [19] He applies the theories set forth in the *Arts d'Amour* by showing us characters who act according to the rules of these treatises. The second part, by Jean de Meung, is its very antithesis.

This second part is of major significance because it provides the stimulus for an attack by the first woman to take an active part in the defense of her sex, Christine de Pisan. Italian by birth, French by adoption, she is the first female to protest the treatment of women in writing, and to defend them from Jean de Meung's denunciations. It is in the *Roman de la Rose* that she finds grounds for complaint against those she considers slanderers of women. As defender of her sex, she writes *L'Epitre au Dieu d'Amours,* in which she lauds women and refutes their adversaries. The poem begins with an address to the God of Love by all types of women who complain to him of the cruelty of men:

>   Car tout homme doit avoir le cuer tendre
>   Envers femme qui a tout homme est mere
>   Et ne lui est ne diverse n'amere,
>   Ainçois souefve, doulce et amiable,
>   A son besoing piteuse et secourable,
>   Qui tant lui a fait et fait de services,
>   Et de qui tant les œuvres sont propices
>   A corps d'omme souefvement nourrir;
>   A son naistre. au vivre et au morir,
>   Lui sont femmes aidans et secourables,
>   Et piteuses, doulces et serviables.
>   ... dis-je que trop se desnature
>   Homme qui dit diffame, ne laidure,

---

[19] Guillaume de Lorris et Jean de Meung, *Le Roman de la Rose* (Paris, 1968), p. 2.

Ne reproche de femme en la blasment,
Ne une, ne deux, ne tout generaulment. [20]

Christine de Pisan played a significant role in the "Querelle," as she condemned the clergymen who filled young students with scorn for all women. She pleaded her case in the name of the God of Love, and established herself as the champion of the female sex. In *La Femme et le féminisme avant la Révolution,* Léon Abensour claims that Christine de Pisan was the first to develop the feminist cause with the same spirit and method as modern defenders of women's rights. He sees her *Trésor des dames* and *Cité des dames* as the first expression of feminism as we know it. [21]

---

[20] Christine de Pisan, *Œuvres Poétiques,* ed. Maurice Roy (Paris, 1891), II, pp. 6-7.
[21] Léon Abensour, *La Femme et le féminisme avant la Révolution* (Paris, 1923), pp. v-vi.

CHAPTER II

THE ROLE OF WOMEN
DURING THE FRENCH RENAISSANCE

Montaigne's views about women cannot be isolated from the philosophical context of the Renaissance. In both direct and indirect manners, he was probably aware of the image of the woman held by his predecessors and contemporaries. As far as his antifeminist remarks are concerned, there exists a tradition in which he inserts himself and which he, then, pursues and modifies. When he does speak favorably of women, his words must also be examined in terms of their contemporary effect and the influence of existing currents of thought.

The vituperation of women continues to be a prevalent theme in the literature of the sixteenth century, as one may see in the works of Jean de Nevizan, Gratien Dupont and Tiraqueau; the conception of the woman remains, to a certain extent, medieval. The most important aspect of this abuse is the unquestioned authority of the husband, legal head of the household. He considers himself the absolute owner of both the body and soul of his wife, and the core of this belief can be found in Renaissance literature.

R. de Maulde la Clavière delves into the psychology of domestic life in the sixteenth century; according to him, it was the man who usually complained of marriage because he could not forget "that by setting up an establishment... his chains appeared to him... the sign of a monotonous, unvarying servitude."[1] In that epoch we

---

[1] R. de Maulde la Clavière, *The Women of the Renaissance*, trans. George Herbert Ely (New York, 1905), p. 112.

find in France husbands who envisaged the essential element of wedlock in money. The utilitarian notion of the marriage contract of the Middle Ages was still evident in the Renaissance. "Marriage was a transaction..., a business partnership, a grave material union of interests, rank, and social responsibilities, sanctified by the close personal association of the partners."[2]

Indeed, very frequently the best marriages were negotiated by intermediaries, more or less obliging relatives or friends. Girls were sometimes married in advance and by proxy. At the most basic level, the woman was regarded as her husband's subject. We shall see how this notion filtered into Montaigne's own relationship with his wife.

It may safely be said that Renaissance writers as well as medieval ones exhibited contradictory views with regard to women; on closer analysis, however, we may conclude that a sharp anti-feminist feeling remained. We learn from Maurice Valency that "the idea that women are nuisances and half-wits established itself most firmly in our cultural pattern during the very years in which there flowered most abundantly the poetry of woman-worship."[3] Once again, it would be germane to question whether this "worship" was really of the woman or of some literary convention which was ultimately to the woman's disadvantage because it was so far from her reality.

Screech tells us about the antifeminism of priests and monks, a universal medieval tradition which, unlike Platonic poetry, focuses quite sharply on everyday realities: "It was... normal to propagate the ideal of celibacy by dwelling on the foulness of women, the cursed burden of squalling children and the misery of cuckoldom."[4]

The natural result of this attitude was that women had become accustomed to a derivative and passive life and they lacked the courage to confront a society constituted to prevent them from giving effective expression to their ideas; no channels existed through which a group of women could be heard. For the most part, women were incapable of fighting France's laws, customs and educational system. This becomes apparent in the plaintive confes-

---

[2] *Ibid.*, p. 22.
[3] Valency, p. 3.
[4] Screech, p. 3.

sion of Hélisenne de Crenne's autobiographical novel, *Les Angoysses douloureuses qui procèdent d'amours* (Lyon, 1538).

Nevertheless, the Renaissance was a transitional epoch which also affected the condition of women. The period to which the appellation Renaissance is affixed really began in Italy with Dante and Petrarch in the fourteenth century, at least in its first lineaments, and reached France in the late fifteenth century. By the time that France decided to move ahead, the women of Italy had already proven able to transform themselves. Increased commerce with Italy brought new ideas into France and the Italian conceptions had their share in affecting current French opinions about women. Indeed, the discussions of women's place in high society, like much else, came to France from Italy. We should be aware that several of the women in the upper strata of Italian society stood on a footing of equality with men, at least educationally. According to Jacob Burckhardt, "the Italian, at the time of the Renaissance, felt no scruple in putting sons and daughters alike under the same course of literary and even philological instruction." [5]

Baldassare Castiglione's *The Book of the Courtier* sheds light in this context. It raises the Renaissance question of women's place in the court, and expounds the Platonic doctrine of their equality with men in love. By establishing the woman as a courtier in her own right, Castiglione makes her equal to the man, and while endowing her with perfection, he offers her an important role in society. However, were we to examine the nature of this role, we would find that she has not lost her fundamental image of servant and ornament, eager to please and to obey. She must still be "a good huswief," she must "entertein all kinde of men," she must be "chaste, wise and courteise," and discreet rather than frank. [6] Of course, we must bear in mind that these qualities are as desirable for the men of the time as for the women; both are set up as courtiers, which means literally, servants to the prince. Nevertheless, the woman's function is still the less direct and the more decorative of the two.

---

[5] Jacob Burckhardt, *The Civilization of the Renaissance in Italy*, trans. S.G.C. Middlemore (London, 1960), p. 204.

[6] Baldassare Castiglione, *The Book of the Courtier*, trans. Sir Thomas Hoby (New York, 1967), p. 217.

How then did it come about that women were able to assume an important role in France? "La Querelle des femmes" was one long debate in Renaissance literature over the status of women. It was during the course of this quarrel that the arguments "pro" and "con" were first formulated, arguments which were to reappear in times to come. Platonic arguments were freely used to defend feminist positions in the sixteenth century.

Renaissance "platonic feminists" took their ideas from Ficino's interpretation of Plato in a mystical Christian sense. They attributed the higher love to the love of men and women. Ficino exalted love, preaching the love of love itself in his *Marsilio Ficino Sopra Lo Amore O Ver' Convito Di Platone* (Firenze, 1544). The consequences of these views were to be of great importance in the conception of love in France during the sixteenth century.

When we speak of the Renaissance in France and the role of women in that era, we must remember the role played by Queen Anne de Bretagne, the wife of Charles VIII and Louis XII who brought women into the court for the purpose of teaching them how to gain the respect of the opposite sex. It was under her influence that writers such as Héroët began publishing works that exalted love and women. This began the rise of the literature that defended women, as represented by such writers as Agrippa, Billon, Bouchard, and Mademoiselle de Gournay.

A large number of authors were prepared to write on both sides of the controversy. It would be impossible to discuss the problem of feminism as treated in the first half of the sixteenth century without mentioning the part played by Erasmus. According to Screech, Erasmus was "amongst the most outspoken champions of marriage and the moral rights of women."[7] He represents a decided advance in his thinking over the majority of his contemporaries. In the *Colloquies of Erasmus,* for example, we find "The Abbot and the Learned Lady," in which he asserts the woman's capacity for the same type of education as the man. We are told that "women are just as capable of learning as men are, that learning is not morally dangerous, and that it is no hindrance to domestic concord."[8]

---

[7] Screech, p. 14.
[8] *The Colloquies of Erasmus,* trans. Craig. G. Thompson (Chicago, 1965), p. 218.

Although such a view still limits the woman to her subservient role, we must remember that advocating education for her is rather advanced for the time. And it accords her a mental capacity that had previously been denied to her.

"*La Querelle des femmes*"

It is only with the exposure of new ideas and the preponderant influence of females in society, with the Renaissance and Reformation, that a "Querelle" would appear in the name of woman, as announced long before by Christine de Pisan in *Le Trésor de la cité des dames* (Paris, 1497).

From this point on, books defending women enjoyed the greatest success. While the opposite view had long been taken for granted, the champions of the fair sex were now the only ones to be heard, if we trust the reader's reception of the *Déclamation de la noblesse et préexcellence du sexe féminin* (Anvers, 1530). This little book by Corneille Agrippa de Nettesheim became the most famous of its kind; it was imitated in all Europe by those who had taken part in the "Querelle." In his treatise, the author discusses the paradox of the superiority of the female sex over the "strong sex." He introduces ideas which we shall find again in feminist writings of the following centuries. The favorable way that *De nobilitate* was received is explained by the fact that the sixteenth century reader was more inclined to accept praise of women;[9] old prejudices were discarded. The reaction against the Middle Ages, the rebirth of platonism, and humanism itself created an atmosphere from which women could profit.

Agrippa may well be called an ardent feminist, for he not only defended the sex against its maligners, but he went much further and demanded for it significant political privileges. Georges Ascoli goes so far as to call him the true father of feminism.[10]

Another important book for the "Querelle des femmes" and one which caused much criticism pro and con was written by Gratien du Pont, Sieur de Drusac, *Controverses des sexes masculin*

---

[9] Telle, p. 54.
[10] Georges Ascoli, "Essai sur l'histoire des idées féministes en France du XVIe siècle à la Révolution," *Revue de Synthèse Historique* (Juillet à Decembre, 1906), p. 36.

et féminin (Toulouse, 1543), and is virulent in its attack upon women. He considers them inferior and incapable of worthy acts. His conclusion is that all women are fools; this time however, his book caused many to come to the defense of women.

Among them was Jean Bouchet, rhetorician of Poitou. In his epistle *Aux hommes et femmes mariez* (*Epistres morales*, 1545) he takes the point of view of Christine de Pisan: that those who slandered women were themselves immoral. Like Erasmus, he believes that social rank should be the determining factor in the education of women. We can see that discrimination continues to exist, but now the basis is economic rather than sexual.

Let us now examine woman herself. The woman of 1550 demands the respect of men, the fidelity of the husband and the right to study. This is, therefore, a "Querelle des femmes" in the name of her rights in addition to her duties as wife. Limitations are, of course, abundant. The sixteenth century woman played no part in economic life. It is useless to speak of young girls, since they were married while hardly out of childhood, from the age of twelve. Only the married woman or widow could take part in social life; or else the nun, since there was but one choice for women: marriage or the convent.

Hélisenne de Crenne, author of the autobiographical novel, *Les Angoysses douloureuses qui procèdent d'amours,* is the only woman to appear as a champion of her sex in the first part of the century. The heroine of the novel is a married woman who has a lover. This book functions as a defense; we hear the heroine's side of the story, especially insofar as she is her husband's victim. Not atypical of his time, he sees her as a base, lustful creature: "Mon mary commença à m'increper et injurier, en disant: 'O meschante et malheureuse creature remplie d'iniquité, qui ne desire que l'execution de ton appetit desordonné, comment t'ose tu trouver en ma presence?'"[11] We learn from Louis Loviot that Hélisenne was separated from her husband who reproached her for having published the *Angoysses* only to spread the scandal of her private life.[12] Hélisenne based her writings on a fundamental belief in the goodness of

---

[11] Hélisenne de Crenne, *Les Angoysses douloureuses qui procèdent d'amours,* ed. Paule Demats (Paris, 1968), p. 34.

[12] Louis Loviot, "Hélisenne de Crenne," *Revue des livres anciens* (Paris, 1917), pp. 142-143.

women. In her subsequent *Epistres familieres et invectives* (Paris, 1539), she speaks out in favor of the educational rights of her fellow women.

But the "Querelle" was characterized by more than personal defense and it tied in with other movements. Indeed, in 1540 we find the brilliant but short-lived triumph of neo-platonic philosophy concurrent with a repetition of the discussion of women. Once again, the Querelle became the center of conversation. And it was also at this time that Marguerite de Navarre composed the *Heptaméron* (Paris, 1560).

Though unfinished, the *Heptaméron* could be considered as the first literary attempt to examine the relations between the two sexes. We should be aware of the danger of placing the collection of tales in an isolated feminist context; the work is dominated by Christian thought and the inherent quality of women is a function of the fact that all human beings are equal before God. Men are no better than women, but both are nothing in the face of the All-Powerful. The *Heptaméron* is therefore paradoxical in its significance: at no point does Marguerite actually embark upon the defense of her sex, yet there is an implicit condemnation of anti-feminism. The Queen proves severe with both sexes, but the males receive the sharper verbal lashing. Up to that time, it was always the man who complained of treatment accorded him. But now we hear the woman's voice, especially through the character of Parlamente, expressing her justifiable complaints against him: "Car ung homme qui se venge de son ennemy et le tue pour ung desmentir en est estimé plus gentil compagnon; aussy est-il quant il en ayme une douzaine avecq sa femme. Mais l'honneur des femmes a autre fondement: c'est douceur, patience et chasteté." [13] We can readily see that Marguerite de Navarre's work is a significant document for the history of feminism, despite the fact that the qualities Parlamente attributes to women are no longer as desirable as they once were.

Other writers flocked around this influential woman, and adopted the Platonic doctrine of love. We could say that the second part of the sixteenth century begins with the publication of *La Parfaicte amye* (Paris, 1542) of Antoine Héroët, which has as its subject the theory of Platonic love. We must understand that this was a period

---

[13] Marguerite de Navarre, *L'Heptaméron* (Paris, 1964), p. 301.

in which Platonism dominated. Though this philosophy contains a variety of aspects, the woman is still the disembodied idealization of the Middle Ages, in the service of a love which remains beyond her. Since the Platonic conception of woman had her embodying the essential Idea, love for her was really love of her spirit.

La Parfaicte amye was a reply to a rather cynical poem by La Borderie, entitled *L'Amye de court* (Paris, 1541). The latter reflects the atmosphere of certain areas of the court and large cities, and centers on a coquette. As an attack on love, or at least the kind of love which exists outside the noblest sentiments, it serves as a target for Héroët. *La Parfaicte amye* is about a woman who talks about her lovers but concentrates on the metaphysical aspects of her love. The poet places himself in the feminist camp by introducing a certain woman who devotes herself to love. Reaction to the work was widespread. Abel Lefranc tells us that " 'la querelle des femmes'... trouva dans l'apparition de *L'Amye de Court* de Borderie, puis de *La Parfaicte Amye,* en 1542, l'occasion de se rouvrir et de remettre aux prises les défenseurs et les adversaires éternels du sexe féminin." [14]

One of Héroët's followers was Maurice Scève, leader of the Renaissance movement at Lyon and author of *Délie* (Lyon, 1544). The woman to whom he addressed *Délie* is supposed to have been Pernette de Guillet; she is the first bourgeois woman poet whose works have been preserved (*Les Rymes de la gentille et vertueuse dame Pernette du Guillet,* Lyon, 1545). In addition to being an excellent poet in her own right, Pernette represents the characteristic attitude of her sex, desirous of becoming well-educated.

Education for women was advocated by such men as Erasmus; nevertheless, it was not a general understanding. Although we have on the one hand Louise Labé (*Débat de folie et d'amour,* 1555) who believed that her sex can equal if not exceed the male sex in learning, women did not receive the opportunity to prove her claim.

It is important to note that some of the writers of the century who advocate education for women, such as Erasmus or Agrippa d'Aubigné, do not believe that it should exist for all women. It

---

[14] Abel Lefranc, *Rabelais: Etudes sur Gargantua, Pantagruel, le Tiers Livre* (Paris, 1953), p. 264.

was limited to women of noble birth who needed instruction in order to compete with the learned Italian women at court.

In general, the literature during the reign of François Ier became an essentially courtly literature. In the king's entourage, women occupied an increasingly important position; therefore, the popular writings of the time, inspired by women and works destined for a female public, were to change their tone. They avoided some of the brutality that characterized this kind of literature in the Middle Ages; their aim was to please the woman.

It is undeniable that at the end of the century women played a more important part in society than at the beginning. This growth in influence was due to the ability of certain leading women, those celebrated by Brantôme in the *Vies des dames illustres*. He recognized the varied abilities of women and approved of their application in society, acknowledging in certain famous figures a feminine combination of power and grace.

What was the position of Rabelais vis-à-vis the "Querelle des femmes"? François Billon, the defender of women in *Le Fort inexpugnable de l'honneur du sexe féminin* (Paris, 1555) refers to Rabelais as part of the antifeminist movement; we find in Lefranc's *Rabelais* that Nevizan, Jean Boccace and le seigneur de Drussac are "parmi les trois prisonniers qui personnifient au premier chef le mouvement antiféministe. Ces trois personnages sont, à ses yeux, — avec Rabelais, — les représentants les plus notoires, les plus dangereux et les plus caracterisés du groupe des adversaires de l'honneur féminin." [15]

Rabelais is presented by Billon as the adversary of women who "les a menés au combat pendant la mémorable controverse; son *Tiers Livre* est directement et obstinément visé." [16] In this famous book, Panurge seeks advice as to whether or not he should marry. When we read these chapters closely, we cannot help but notice the scornful conception of women presented.

But on the other hand, Rabelais glorifies woman in his abbaye de Thélème, where "le tout estoit faict selon l'arbitre des dames," [17] and where men and women coexist peacefully. According to Lefranc,

---

[15] *Ibid.*, p. 270.
[16] *Ibid.*, p. 315.
[17] François Rabelais, *Œuvres Complètes* (Paris, 1962), I, p. 202.

such an attitude is necessary to his antimonastic conception, though he is not praising them for themselves.[18] And it is also necessary to emphasize that Rabelais devotes his attention to the training of boys and says nothing about that of girls, as if he considers it unnecessary.

An illuminating study in this context is Saulnier's *Le Dessein de Rabelais*. This perceptive critic agrees that misogyny is not absent from the *Tiers Livre,* citing such examples as Sœur Fessue (who allowed herself to be caressed by a monk because she was afraid of breaking the law of silence by calling for help), and the nuns of Fontevrault.[19] Nevertheless, he also finds that Rabelais acknowledges superior women: "La dédicace à Marguerite de Navarre suffit à l'indiquer."[20] Furthermore, woman in general retains a certain dignity for Rabelais in her capacity to propagate. Maternity and "un mérite tout personnel" combine to render woman slightly noble: "Elle n'est pas seulement là pour la 'perpétuité de l'espèce humaine,' mais aussi pour la 'sociale délectation de l'homme.' Consolation domestique et entretènement de ménage..."[21]

Woman is seen as useful, and if she is dangerous, it is from fragility rather than viciousness. Although Rabelais depicts her as having a marked taste for forbidden fruit, Saulnier reminds us that this tendency can be gently controlled: "Ne l'oublions pas: Rabelais n'avait pas, au départ, une si triste idée de la femme. Il la voyait esprit, capable de bonne doctrine."[22] Saulnier sees Rabelais' anti-feminism as a reaction to those who, "contre nature," were placing woman on a pedestal:

> C'est parce qu'il ne voulait à aucun prix instituer la femme-déesse, que Rabelais se durcit parfois dans l'idée inverse.[23]

Therefore, if we take the totality of Rabelais' work into consideration, along with the critics' conflicting judgments, we find that we cannot truthfully label him either feminist or antifeminist.

---

[18] Lefranc, p. 280.
[19] V. L. Saulnier, *Le Dessein de Rabelais* (Paris, 1957), p. 79.
[20] *Ibid.,* p. 80.
[21] *Ibid.,* p. 81.
[22] *Ibid.,* p. 85.
[23] *Ibid.,* p. 87.

Perhaps the safest thing we can claim is that since he was writing within the context of the Querelle, and since it could not help but enter into his writings, he reflects the attitudes of his time. Though he never condemns women as a whole, he doesn't portray them entirely favorably either.

As we can see, the majority of thinkers, writers and poets of the sixteenth century took side actively on the "Querelle des femmes." Even if they sided against women, their very participation indicated how important the feminist question was becoming. With all this attention, women tended to play an increasingly large role in society.

Chapter III

INFLUENCES OF ANTIQUITY

A great writer like Rabelais or Montaigne is a mirror of his age, reflecting existing patterns of thought while forming new ones. Montaigne's concepts of womanhood are connected with attitudes of his time, and just as the Renaissance held a reverence for the Ancients, so his views had their roots in antiquity. We need only note the abundance of quotations from the Classics to see the extent to which antiquity permeates the *Essais*.

To understand why Montaigne had to model himself after the Ancients, we must remember that the Renaissance was a time when no writer would allow himself to display his talents without showing his debt to the venerated names of the past. As for Montaigne, he combined an assimilation of this material with his own originality. Hugo Friedrich tells us that "l'essai de Montaigne, par contact direct avec les sources antiques, mais encouragé par le goût de l'époque, réunit les genres de la lettre et du dialogue, parents par leur origine comme par leur développement, et en crée une forme nouvelle." [1]

One cannot overemphasize Montaigne's great admiration for the Classics and his extensive knowledge of the ancient writers. We learn in *Thoughts from Montaigne* that as a child of eight, he translated Ovid, and became so enchanted with poetry that he passed on to Virgil, Terence and Plato. [2] The love of the Latin

---

[1] Hugo Friedrich, *Montaigne*, trans. Robert Rovini (Paris, 1968), p. 375.
[2] Montaigne, *Thoughts from Montaigne*, ed. C. de la Warr (Boston: L. C. Page & Company, 1905), p. 9.

tongue was very strong in him; he spoke the language before French: "... Latin, qui m'a esté donné pour maternel." [3]

The first phase of his literary career is characterized by the presence of Seneca, and may be termed his Stoical period. Montaigne gradually emancipated himself from this phase under the influence of Plutarch, whose *Lives* and *Moral Works* he read in Amyot's translation. The last and most important part of the *Essais* constitutes his Skeptical period, with its extensive borrowing from Sextus Empiricus. Nevertheless, Seneca is still present; Pierre Villey goes so far as to note over a hundred quotations from Seneca. [4]

However, we should not let the obvious Stoic influence eclipse the Epicurean aspect of the *Essais*. As A. Armaingaud puts it, "oui, il est très vrai que Montaigne adopte avec enthousiasme les 22 sentences de Sénèque placées par lui aux chapitres XIV et XLII du livre I et au chapitre I du livre II des *Essais*. Mais ce n'est pas un souffle stoïcien, c'est un souffle épicurien qui passe par ces chapitres." [5] Armaingaud feels that Montaigne was always an Epicurean, beginning with his so-called early phase in 1572 and culminating in his mature efforts through 1592. [6]

Although the primary philosophical thrust of the *Essais* is towards moderation, Montaigne constantly reminds us to fill our lives with as much joy as possible; he tells us, "il faut courir le mauvais et se rassoir au bon." [7] In his awareness of the brevity of life, he makes the individual responsible for life's plenitude and beauty: "Je la jouys au double des autres, car la mesure en la jouyssance depend du plus ou moins d'application que nous y prestons ... à mesure que la possession du vivre est plus courte, il me la faut rendre plus profonde et plus pleine." [8] This attitude to life

---

[3] Michel de Montaigne, *Essais* (Paris: Editions Garnier Frères, 1962), Tome II, Livre II, p. 40. All subsequent quotations are from this edition and will be designated by volume, book and page.

[4] Pierre Villey, *Les Sources et l'évolution des Essais de Montaigne* (Paris, 1908), II, p. 289.

[5] Michel de Montaigne, *Œuvres Complètes*, notes by A. Armaingaud (Paris, 1924), I, p. 118.

[6] *Ibid.*, p. 128.

[7] Montaigne, T. II, L, III, p. 572.

[8] *Ibid.*, p. 572.

emphasizes the present but its source lies deep in the past; many Ancients had also held it.

Montaigne himself acknowledges classical superiority; he declares, "... les productions de ces riches et grandes âmes du temps passé sont bien loing au delà de l'extreme estendue de mon imagination et souhaict. Leurs escris ... m'estonnent et transsissent d'admiration." [9] There seems to be no question that his general views on life take root in antiquity.

In exploring the classical influences on Montaigne, we can begin by viewing him in his totality, that is, as a man who acknowledges the conflicting facets of his nature. On the one hand, he is conscious of his sensuality; he calls himself one of "ceux en qui le corps peut beaucoup." [10] On the other hand, he experiences the need to control his passion. In the essay entitled "De Mesnager sa volonté," Montaigne shows his desire to guard against the assault of the passions. He prefers to avoid rather than brave them: "Avec bien peu d'effort j'arreste ce premier branle de mes emotions, et abandonne le subject qui me commence à poiser, et avant qu'il m'emporte." [11]

Considering his extensive use of quotations from Catullus and Seneca, one might say that he sees himself (and man in general) as embodying the dichotomy between passion and Stoic reserve, though he is obviously determined to subjugate his internal Catullus to his Seneca. As he declares, "qui n'eut tenu un peu en bride cette naturelle violence de leur desir par la crainte et honneur dequoy on les a pourveues, nous estions diffamez." [12] Within this context, the importance of the woman becomes apparent, because at a most basic level it is she who is at the source of Montaigne's passion.

In this struggle against passion, Montaigne once again reveals his deep classical roots. Although certain ancient writers relegate love to the realms of domestic comfort or sensual pleasure, Denis de Rougemont attributes to the Ancients the supposition that "the profane passion is something absurd, ... a sickness of the soul." [13]

---

[9] *Ibid.*, T. II, L. II, p. 37.
[10] Montaigne, T. II, L. III, p. 245.
[11] *Ibid.*, p. 463.
[12] *Ibid.*, p. 282.
[13] Denis de Rougemont, *Love in the Western World* (New York, 1956), p. 282.

Passion becomes a sacred madness, as in *Antigone* or Lucretius.

To a certain extent, Montaigne seems to be in agreement with this view. We should be aware that love and passion are used interchangeably in the *Essais*, thereby stressing love's essentially physical aspect. Its irrationality must be controlled or at least tempered by a Stoic reserve; he tells us that even as a young boy, he tried to avoid the onslaught of love: "Comme, estant jeune, je m'opposais au progrez de l'amour que je sentoy trop avancer sur moy, et estudiois qu'il ne me fut si aggreable qu'il vint à me forcer en fin et captiver du tout à sa mercy, j'en use de mesure à toutes autres occasions où ma volonté se prend avec trop d'appetit; je me penche à l'opposite de son inclination." [14] He then goes on to show us the worthiness of Seneca as a model. He takes from his *Epistres* the example of the philosopher Panetius who told a young man about love, "ne nous engageons en chose si esmeuë et violente, qui nous escllave à autruy et nous rende contemptibles à nous." [15] We shall see how this conception of enslavement to others gains primary significance for Montaigne.

Here we should be aware of Armaingaud's Preface to the *Essais* especially when he makes an important point by reminding us of Montaigne's essentially contradictory nature: "Il a, toute sa vie, fait effort pour combattre ses inclinations et ses passions, et cependant il affirme à plusieurs reprises qu'il n'a jamais rien fait pour atteindre ce but, et qu'il est resté ce qu'il a toujours été." [16] Montaigne himself actually admits to this: "Je donne à mon ame tantost un visage, tantost un autre, selon le costé où je la couche. Si je parle diversement de moy, c'est que je me regarde diversement. Toutes les contrarietez s'y trouvent." [17]

As long as a certain distance exists between Montaigne and women, he feels more free to indulge himself in admiration. He had a fine aesthetic sense and yielded to the cult of physical beauty as any artist of the Renaissance did. His eyes always searched for charm in the face and body of women, avid to meet "all the beautiful gentlewomen of Rome ... for in Italy they do not mask

---

[14] Montaigne, T. II, L. III, p. 460.
[15] *Ibid.*, pp. 321-322.
[16] Montaigne, *Œuvres Complètes*, I, p. 101.
[17] Montaigne, T. I, L. II, p. 369.

themselves as in France, and show themselves with faces quite uncovered ... commonly they are more attractive." [18] We find in his *Journal de Voyage* that Montaigne was in Rome at carnival time. He was astonished by the women, who were "very beautiful, with straw hats ... and well dressed for village women." [19] In Florence, he "went alone for fun to see the women who let themselves be seen by anyone who wants. I saw the most famous." [20] Wherever he went, he observed women with an admiring eye.

Thanks to the pervasive classical atmosphere of the *Essais,* we are able to become acquainted with yet another discussion of love, asserting important implications about women. In Book II, Chapter XV, Montaigne quotes Lycurgus as reported in *Plutarch's Lives*: "Pour tenir l'amour en haleine, Licurgue ordonna que les mariez de Lacedemone ne se pourroient prattiquer qu'à la desrobée, et que ce seroit pareille honte de les rencontrer couchés ensemble, qu'avecques d'autres." [21] So here we see Montaigne dreaming of sieges and conquests in love. The difficulties of rendez-vous, the danger of suprises, the shame of the day after excite him: "La difficulté des assignations, ... c'est ce qui donne pointe à la sauce." [22] He tells us that this is the general course of things, that difficulties increase value: "La rigueur des maistresses est ennuyeuse, mais l'aisance et la facilité l'est, à dire verité, encore plus." [23] What we can deduce from these lines is that Montaigne was equating love with a game — a dangerous one perhaps, but still a game. This possibility is supported later by his notion that love is "un sot desduit qui ne le ferait valoir par fantaisie et par cherté" [24] and that "plus il y a de marches et degrez, plus il y a de hauteur et d'honneur au dernier siege." [25] This view can be interpreted as an attempt on his part to guard against the deeper hold of passion for which we have already seen his disdain. On another level, it is

---

[18] Montaigne, "Travel Journal," *The Complete Works of Montaigne,* trans. Donald Frame (Stanford, 1967), p. 946.
[19] *Ibid.,* p. 980.
[20] *Ibid.,* p. 1006.
[21] Montaigne, T. II, L. II, p. 9.
[22] *Ibid.,* p. 10.
[23] *Ibid.,* p. 11.
[24] *Ibid.,* T. II, L. III, p. 298.
[25] *Ibid.,* p. 309.

a defensive reduction of the woman to a plaything — if she is a challenge, she is worthwhile; if she is easy, she isn't worth the trouble; she needs the game to enhance her. By treating the woman lightly with this kind of generalization, Montaigne becomes less vulnerable to the irrational and powerful love that he wishes to avoid.

If we move to the chapter "Sur des vers de Virgile," we find one of the keys to Montaigne's view of women, and the role of classical influence therein. If we remember that Montaigne read Virgil at an early age, we readily realize that the Roman writer's attitudes probably laid a groundwork for the future course of his thought. It is therefore essential to understand the characterization of women in *The Aeneid*, especially because Montaigne alludes to a portion of this poem himself. He praises Virgil's art in the eighth book, where we find this beautiful expression of passion:

> Dixerat, et niveis hinc atque hinc diva lacertis
> Cunctantem amplexu molli fovet. Ille repente
> Accepit solitam flammam, nousque medullas
> Intravit calor, et labefacta per ossa cucurrit.
> Non secus atque olim tonitru cum rupta corusco
> Ignea rima micans percurrit lumine nimbos.
> . . . . Ea verba loquutus,
> Optatos dedit amplexus, placidumque petivit
> Conjugis infusus gremio per membra soporem. [26]

It is not enough to perceive Venus in her sexuality; we must also return this passage to the context of *The Aeneid* to find that she is using her physical powers to obtain something from her husband. She embraces him "since Vulcan complied not at once." [27] Here, passion is obviously not depicted as the "madness" discussed earlier; however, if we read between the lines, its hold is a powerful

---

[26] Montaigne, T. II, L. III, p. 272. ("Since Vulcan complied not at once, the goddess softly embraced him in snowdrift arms, caressing him here and there. Of a sudden, he caught the familiar spark and felt the old warmth darting into his marrow, coursing right through his body, melting him; just as it often happens a thunderclap starts a flaming rent which ladders the dark cloud, a quivering streak of fire.... He gave his wife the love he was aching to give her; then he sank into soothing sleep, relaxed upon her breast." *The Aeneid of Virgil*, trans. C. Day Lewis [New York, 1953], p. 191.)

[27] *The Aeneid of Virgil*, p. 191.

one through which the female goddess gets what she wants from the male god.

Montaigne did not quote the entire passage; for our purposes, the following section is a highly important one. In the midst of their love-making,

> Pleased with her wiles and aware of her beauty,
> Venus could feel them
> Taking effect. Vulcan, in love's undying thrall

agrees to arm the Trojans as she wishes. This would have been in accord with Montaigne's fear of passion, in that it can weaken man's defenses and strengthen the woman's position.

This characterization of the female as essentially sensual (as Montaigne claims, "plus capables et ardentes aux effets de l'amour que nous" [28]) and manipulative also permeates Book IV, the episode of tragic Dido. She is overcome by her passion for Aeneas:

> What value have vows or shrines
> For a woman wild with passion, the while love's flame eats into
> Her gentle flesh and love's wound works silently in her breast?[29]

Their love is shown as the obstacle to their "higher fame,"[30] their responsibility to their kingdoms. When Dido is "overmastered by grief, she conceived a criminal madness,"[31] and uses a trick to get her sister to build a funeral pyre. Mercury then tells Aeneas to depart, for "woman was ever a veering, weathercock creature."[32] Virgil then depicts the ultimate destructiveness of passion: the fire of love that we witnessed with Venus and Vulcan is now the fire of death, as Dido expires in the flames. Maud Bodkin's comment is noteworthy here, especially with regard to what Dido may have represented for Montaigne: "The figure of Dido may express the rebellious passion of love rejected from the socially ordered life of man."[33]

---

[28] Montaigne, T. II, L. III, p. 278.
[29] Virgil, p. 83.
[30] *Ibid.*, p. 87.
[31] *Ibid.*, p. 95.
[32] *Ibid.*, p. 98.
[33] Maud Bodkin, *Archetypal Patterns in Poetry: Psychological Studies of Imagination* (London, 1965), p. 216.

In many literary works of antiquity, passion comes to be associated with the female, in contrast to the rationality and heroism of the male. As Valency notes,

> both in comedy and in tragedy, most official of the Greek genres, women were depicted as enemies of the rational order of society. In Clytemnestra, Medea, Phaedra, and Antigone we see nothing of the passive attitude considered suitable to the Athenian lady. ... Such women were traditionally depicted as passion's slaves; whoever loved them came to grief.[34]

To these major figures of Greek tragedy, we can add names such as Dido, Helen, Andromache and Cassandra in order to comprehend the incredible power that these women possessed. Their capacity, in literature, to affect life and death on a mass scale (as in the case of Helen of Troy) may have led to a need on the part of the male to control this irrational power.

However, keeping in mind that Montaigne's natural and unstructured style allows for contradiction (or rather, seeing more than one side of an issue), we must be aware of other sections of Chapter V of the Third Book. First he quotes Horace's third Ode (VI) on the lasciviousness of young girls:

> Motus doceri gaudet Ionicos
> Matura virgo, et frangitur artubus
> Jam nunc, et incestos amores
> De tenero meditatur ungui.[35]

But a few pages later, he takes responsibility as a male for the sexual appetite of women: "On les leurre, en somme, et acharne par tous moyens; nous eschauffons et incitons leur imagination sans cesse, et puis nous crions au ventre!"[36]

We can see this totality again when he borrows two lines from Juvenal's sixth Satire, famous for its antifeminism:

---

[34] Valency, p. 11.
[35] Montaigne, T. II, L. III, p. 281. (The ripened maid delights to learn/In wanton Ionic dance to turn,/And fondly dreams, when still a child,/Of loves incestuous and wild." *The Complete Works of Montaigne*, p. 651.)
[36] Ibid., p. 286.

> Pone seram, cohibe; sed quis custodiet ipsos
> Custodes? Canta est, et ab illis incipit uxor. [37]

This attack is tempered by the fact that he spends the two preceding pages defending women by proving that it is often the needs of society that engender their moral (or immoral) behavior. And as he states later, "la deffence les incite et convie." [38]

As far as the role of the Classics is concerned, we can find in Catullus the culminating influence for Montaigne's views of passion and women. For one thing, he uses a quotation from the Latin poet's # LXVIIIb to support his contention that jealousy is strongest in women:

> Sæpe etiam Juno, maxima cælicolum,
> Conjugis in culpa flagravit quotidiana. [39]

More significantly, upon reading the *Carmina*, we find that his famous "Lesbia" is a perfidious, unfaithful and cruel woman who turns Catullus' love into suffering. It is from Catullus that Montaigne learns that love is "une passion insupportable." [40] He quotes from another of his poems to demonstrate how passion attacks both the body and soul:

> Misero quod omnes
> Eripit sensus mihi. Nam simul te,
> Lesbia, aspexi, nihil est super mi
> Quod loquar amens.
> Lingua sed torpet, tenuis sub artus
> Flamma dimanat, sonitu suopte
> Tinniunt aures, gemina, tegentur
> Lumina nocte. [41]

---

[37] *Ibid.*, p. 296. ("Put on a lock, confine her. But then who will guard/The guards themselves? Your wife is shrewd; with them she'll start." *The Complete Works of Montaigne*, p. 661.)

[38] *Ibid.*, p. 298.

[39] *Ibid.*, p. 291. ("For often Juno, mistress of the gods,/Burns at her husband's daily escapades." *The Complete Works of Montaigne*, p. 658.)

[40] Montaigne, T. I, L. I, p. 9.

[41] *Ibid.*, pp. 9-10. ("Alas, my senses, dazed,/Are snatched away. For soon as I have gazed/On thee, Lesbia, my wits depart amazed,/I can say nothing./My tongue is numb, a subtle fire runs round/Throughout my every limb, my ears resound/With ringing all their own, both eyes are drowned/In blackest night." *Complete Works*..., p. 7.)

Love is seen as the instrument which reduces the poet to a slave and gives power to the woman. Montaigne finds that in succumbing to the intense joy of love, Catullus lost himself to the control of a vile woman.

What is Montaigne's answer to this problem? One solution which lessens the threat posed by the woman is to see love as nothing more than a physical event, Eros no more than a bodily need. In the same chapter, Montaigne states, "l'amour n'est autre chose que la soif de cette jouyssance en un subject desiré, ny Venus autre chose que le plaisir à descharger ses vases." [42] Yet, this does not prove to be an entirely valid path. In his typically paradoxical manner, Montaigne later finds, "j'ay horreur d'imaginer mien un corps privé d'affection" [43] and "ce n'est pas une passion simplement corporelle." [44]

Montaigne's see-saw between these two views of love is pushed to its limits when he says that philosophy "nous ordonne de prendre un object qui satisface simplement au besoing du corps; qui n'esmeuve point l'ame," [45] and proceeds to ask in the next paragraph, "pouvons nous pas dire qu'il n'y a rien en nous, ... purement ny corporel ny spirituel, et que injurieusement nous dessirons un homme tout vif?" [46] It is not enough for him to possess a woman's body; in his own totality, he desires her soul as well, but this, of course, does not entail the woman's possession of his soul.

Since passion was seen as embodied in the woman (as in the image of Dido), one of the things Montaigne learned from the Ancients was a wariness of the power of her sensuality. As Bodkin perceives, "... the felt significance of the unending warfare Dido prophesied would lie in that inner conflict ... between passionate feelings and the need for strong defence against them." [47]

---

[42] *Ibid.*, T. II, L. III, p. 305.
[43] *Ibid.*, p. 311.
[44] *Ibid.*, p. 315.
[45] *Ibid.*, p. 323.
[46] *Ibid.*, p. 323.
[47] Bodkin, p. 199.

CHAPTER IV

MONTAIGNE'S PERSONAL BACKGROUND AND WOMEN

Montaigne's appearance

In exploring the underlying influences that may have led Montaigne to one reaction or another to the question of feminism, we cannot ignore his physical reality, especially because Montaigne himself stresses the importance of the body: "Le corps a une grand'part à nostre estre, il y tient un grand rang." [1] If we accept that our bodies are profoundly significant in the formation of our personalities, our viewpoints, and the style of our interaction with others, we realize that Montaigne's physical form may shed light on his relationship to the women he knew.

We should first explore whether Montaigne possessed the qualities that make a man attractive to women. The question is obviously abstract and general, but Montaigne seems to answer it specifically for us. In Book II, he declares, "or je suis d'une taille un peu au dessoubs de la moyenne. Ce defáut n'a pas seulement de la laideur, mais encore de l'incommodité ... car l'authorité que donne une belle presence et majesté corporelle en est à dire." [2] His words suggest a feeling of inferiority due to his small size, and this sense is intensified when he admits that the "beautez" are for women, but "la beauté de la taille est la seule beauté des hommes." [3]

---

[1] Montaigne, T. II, L. II, p. 40.
[2] *Ibid.*, p. 41.
[3] *Ibid.*, p. 42.

In the same chapter, he informs us, "j'ay au demeurant la taille forte et ramassée; le visage, non pas gras, mais plein; la complexion, entre le jovial et le melancholique, moiennement sanguine et chaude..." [4]

His lack of enthusiasm for his own appearance implies the opinion of other people, since our view of ourselves is rarely separable from how we think others see us. It is safe to assume from the *Essais* that he did not have the "good looks" that would make him an immediate success with women. His physical inferiority may have resulted in coolness, resentment, or even fear of women, based on his exterior self-appraisal.

In addition, Montaigne had difficulty in learning the talents necessary for social intercourse. Whether it was music, dancing, tennis or hunting, he found his body (and consequently, himself) mediocre:

> D'adresse et de disposition, je n'en ay point eu; ... de la musique, ny pour la voix que j'y ay trèsinepte, ny pour les instrumens, on ne m'y a jamais sceu rien apprendre. A la danse, à la paume, à la lutte, je n'y ay peu acquerir qu'une bien fort legere et vulgaire suffisance; à nager, à escrimer, à voltiger et à sauter, nulle du tout. Les mains, je les ay si gourdes que je ne sçay pas escrire seulement pour moy. ... Mes conditions corporelles sont en somme trèsbien accordantes à celles de l'ame. Il n'y a rien d'allegre ... [5]

The critics are in agreement over the kind of restraint that characterizes Montaigne's relationships with women. The early nineteenth century critic, Jean-Baptiste Biot, actually pities Montaigne because he feels that his coldness kept him from being truly happy; he adds that Montaigne's obsessive philosophical self-analysis ultimately robbed him of the joys of life. [6] It might be worthwhile to ask ourselves what would have pushed Montaigne to this preoccupation and whether his immersion in the world of his mind could not have been an attempt to compensate for his lack of pride in the world of his body.

---

[4] *Ibid.*, p. 42.
[5] *Ibid.*, p. 43.
[6] Jean-Baptiste Biot, *Mélanges scientifiques et littéraires* (Paris, 1858), p. 65.

As for Guillaume Guizot, he is convinced that Montaigne must be considered cold and egoistic.[7] Once again, if this is indeed the case, we must consider the possibility that his coldness and egoism are of a defensive nature, based on the threat of a woman's rejection, or as we shall see later, domination.

Montaigne and his mother

Montaigne's mother is conspicuous by her absence in the *Essais*, especially when we consider that his father is a recurring subject of conversation. The fact that Montaigne seems to avoid mention of his mother is significant in a study of his views about women. In focusing on the role of the mother, the dangers of psychologizing are obviously great; but Montaigne himself leads us to such a discussion when he states, "je trouve que nos plus grands vices prennent leur ply des nostre plus tendre enfance."[8] In a similar fashion, we can add that our thought patterns and behavior also have their sources in childhood.[9]

Montaigne's literary treatment of his father is characterized not only by respect, but by enduring affection as well. The male model in Montaigne's early life was evidently a positive influence. According to his son, Pierre Eyquem was a fine man, "... et luy partoit cette humeur d'une grande bonté de nature; il ne fut jamais ame plus charitable et populaire."[10] Montaigne even says of him, "je me glorifie que sa volonté s'exerce encores et agisse par moy. Jà, à Dieu ne plaise que je laisse faillir entre mes mains aucune image de vie que je puisse rendre à un si bon pere!"[11] He also speaks about him in Book II: in describing his father's marriage, he gives

---

[7] Guillaume Guizot, *Montaigne* (Paris, 1899), p. xiii.
[8] Montaigne, T. I, L. I, p. 114.
[9] As Freudian critic Norman O. Brown states, "according to psychoanalytical theory... wisdom directs us to childhood — not only to the immortal wishes of childhood for the substance of things hoped for, but also to the failure of childhood for the cause of our disease" (Norman O. Brown, *Life Against Death: The Psychoanalytical Meaning of History* [Connecticut, 1959], p. 110). And as the master himself puts it, "... whatever the character's later capacity may turn out to be, the effects of the first identifications made in earliest childhood will be general and lasting" (Sigmund Freud, *The Ego and the Id*, trans. Joan Riviere [New York, 1962], p. 21).
[10] Montaigne, T. II, L. III, p. 450.
[11] *Ibid.*, p. 388.

us the pertinent information, such as the date, but neglects to tell us whom he married.[12]

As far as his mother is concerned, we must look elsewhere to learn about her. Armaingaud tells us that she was "une Lopez ou Louppe, de Toulouse, nièce d'un Lopez de Bordeaux. D'origine juive, elle s'était convertie, non pas au catholicisme, mais à la religion réformée, et elle paraît avoir été une maîtresse femme, très entendue et très économe."[13] To find out any more facts about her, it is necessary to refer to archive pieces.

Théophile Malvezin did conscientious research on the subject of Montaigne's mother, even searching in the archives of Haute-Garonne for Pierre Eyquem's marriage contract. He ascertains that Antoinette de Louppes was the daughter of a merchant of Toulouse.[14] All that we know of her age at the time of her marriage is "qu'elle était majeure, âgée de plus de douze ans et de moins de vingt-cinq."[15] Although very little is known about the early years of her married life, we can find some interesting implications about her personality from Eyquem's will.

In 1561 Pierre Eyquem, at sixty-six years of age, writes his will and makes Antoinette executor. Michel was not quite twenty-eight at this time. According to Donald Frame, this "makes Michel the general heir and official head of the family, but provides that his mother be 'mistress ... of my each and every possession, governing them like a good pater-familias.' ... Michel, who showed neither interest in such everyday matters nor knowledge of them, remained a figurehead."[16] As we can see, Pierre Eyquem held his wife in high esteem; he judged her to be intelligent and capable of governing his house. However, in 1567 he made a new will, and died seven years later on June 18, 1568. This will made Montaigne responsible for the upbringing of his sisters, Marie and Leonor.

---

[12] *Ibid.*, T. I, L. II, p. 378.

[13] Montaigne, *Œuvres Complètes*, I, p. 5.

[14] Théophile Malvezin, *Montaigne, son origine, sa famille* (Bordeaux, 1875), p. 122.

[15] Paul Courteault, "La mère de Montaigne," *Revue historique de Bordeaux et du département de la Gironde*, XXVII, numéro 1 (Janvier-Février, 1934), p. 11.

[16] Donald M. Frame, *Montaigne: A Biography* (New York, 1965), p. 24.

These conscientious arrangements shed some light on the relationship between Montaigne and his mother, and also on the character of the latter. Eyquem may have foreseen the case where incompatibility between mother and son (and possibly daughter-in-law) would force a separation. According to Frame, "the agreement suggests ... a struggle for control in what had been her house for forty years but was now his. Whatever the faults on his side, his mother appears as a dominating woman not easily adaptable to any position except mastery." [17]

The foresight of Montaigne's father, the scrupulous care with which all possible future difficulties were envisaged, seem rather significant. It appears that Montaigne's mother was a woman little disposed toward contenting herself with maternal supervision; she liked to dominate. Then, in about 1587, she left the château. There is not enough evidence to prove that her motive for leaving was incompatibility with her son and daughter-in-law; but the possibility does exist.

Frame also suggests that her will of April, 1597 betrays signs of disillusionment and anger. She turned away from Michel's household; her two other sons, Montaigne's brothers, remained the objects of her love. And she made her daughter Leonor her particular inheritor. She reserved all her tenderness for her daughter and grand-daughter, Jeanne de Camain. [18]

Her wishes about her inhumation also deserve notice. Paul Courteault tells us that she didn't particularly care to join her husband at Montaigne, in the tomb of his ancestors. She asked to be buried in Bordeaux. [19] This fact seems indicative of her difficult character. As I mentioned before, Eyquem honored his wife in his will. But as Courteault observes,

> celle-ci paraît avoir trouvé que cet hommage était trop platonique. Femme pratique, peu accessible au prestige des mots, elle rappelle avec fierté qu'elle a été l'active collaboratrice de son mari dans son négoce et ses affaires financières. ... Quelle récompense, en effet, en a-t-elle reçue? [20]

---

[17] *Ibid.*, p. 25.
[18] *Ibid.*, p. 26.
[19] Courteault, numéro 2 (Mars-Avril, 1939), p. 56.
[20] *Ibid.*, pp. 56-57.

Considering the fact that Montaigne spent almost his entire life near his mother (and that she survived him), it seems rather curious that he mentions her only once. This occurs when he tells of the procedures used by his father for his early education: "Mon pere et ma mere y apprindrent assez de Latin pour l'entendre, et en acquirent à suffisance pour s'en servir à la nécessité." [21] Cecil Roth offers the noteworthy hypothesis that Antoinette de Louppe's absence from the *Essais* had something to do with her religious background. He says of Montaigne, "it is now possible to prove what was hitherto only conjectured — that he was on his mother's side of Jewish descent. ... It may well be, indeed, that this was the reason why, in his writings, he refrained from mentioning his mother — a silence which, long considered inexplicable, was perhaps merely discreet." [22]

On the other hand, Paul Stapfer finds nothing questionable in Montaigne's silence about his mother:

> Je ne crois pas ... qu'il y ait rien de très grave à conclure contre Montaigne du silence qu'il a gardé sur sa mère; j'attribue cette singularité moins à quelque vanité nouvelle ou à l'absence d'une dose ordinaire de piété filiale qu'à l'ensemble de sa philosophie, qui dans la formation morale et intellectuelle de l'homme, lui faisait attacher fort peu d'importance au rôle et à l'influence de la femme. [23]

But Stapfer does not resolve the problem of which came first and influenced the other, his philosophy or his feelings about his mother. The nature of a mother's influence is not always easy for a son to articulate, or even to be aware of; this problem is left for a careful reader to explore.

We can safely say that if Montaigne's view of women is paradoxical in the *Essais,* his mother may have helped to form both his pro and anti-female conceptions. On the one hand, we have seen that she was an intelligent and powerful woman with a taste for domination. These characteristics may have kindled both Mon-

---

[21] Montaigne, T. I, L. I, p. 188.
[22] Cecil Roth, *Personalities and Events in Jewish History* (Philadelphia, 1953), pp. 224-225.
[23] Paul Stapfer, *La Famille et les amis de Montaigne* (Paris, 1896), pp. 49-50.

taigne's respect and fear, leading him to admire women at a distance, but be wary of their dominating qualities in personal situations. The fact that the friction between Antoinette and her son was great, coupled with his silence about her, leads one to believe that her influence on her son was not necessarily a positive one; and as Montaigne himself suggested, this early formative presence may have helped to illuminate his later viewpoints. In the possible subsequent association of strong-willed women with images of his mother, he may have been led to a generally negative attitude towards women, especially those who tried to assert themselves. [24]

Montaigne and his wife

In 1565, Montaigne married Françoise de la Chassaigne, daughter of one of his colleagues in the Parliament of Bordeaux. This act stemmed from a desire to please his father, and he looked upon marriage primarily as a social necessity. He actually let himself be married after two years of attempting to divert his grief over the death of his closest friend, La Boétie. He makes no secret of his reasons for marrying: "La plus part de mes actions se conduisent par exemple, non par chois. Toutesfois je ne m'y conviay pas proprement, on m'y mena, et y fus porté par des occasions estrangeres." [25] The *Essais* suggest that he knew only two real affections during his lifetime: for his father and for his beloved La Boétie. His wife was bound to be in some measure the victim of his sorrow for his friend, dead at the age of thirty-three. As Frame tells us, Montaigne had "the inauspicious conviction that marriage ranked far below friendship." [26]

Montaigne made it clear that he had little taste for human ties, and when he took a wife, it was for conventional reasons only. He believed in the institution of the family: "C'est une religieuse liaison

---

[24] Freud speaks of "the root of a mother's importance, unique, without parallel, laid down unalterably for a whole lifetime, as the first and strongest love object and as the prototype of all later love relations-for both sexes" (Sigmund Freud, *An Outline of Psychoanalysis,* trans. James Strachey [New York, 1949], p. 90).

[25] Montaigne, T. II, L. III, p. 276.

[26] Frame, p. 83.

et devote que le mariage ... sa principale fin c'est la generation." [27] Whether he "loved" his wife or not was of no significance for him. Indeed, his heart after La Boétie's death had no room for any sentiment but regret. He cared more for his name and estate than for his children: "On ne se marie pas pour soy, quoi qu'on die; on se marie autant ou plus pour sa posterité, pour sa famille. ... Tout cecy, combien à l'opposite des conventions amoureuses!" [28] It becomes evident in his work that love is not only unnecessary in marriage, but, as in the Middle Ages, incompatible with the institution itself! About love, he exclaims, "plus courte possession nous luy donnons sur nostre vie, mieux nous en valons." [29] That rare phenomenon known as a happy marriage rejects the conditions of love; these conditions constitute for Montaigne no less than an invasion of privacy, a loss of self-control, a passionate and unstable hold. He tells us that "c'est un feu temeraire et volage, ondoyant et divers, feu de fiebvre, subject à accez et remises, et qui ne nous tient qu'à un coing," [30] and that "la jouyssance et la possession appartiennent principalement à l'imagination." [31]

If we turn for a moment to Montaigne's reaction to Virgil, we can learn more about his concept of marriage and the impossibility of love therein. After quoting the beautiful seduction scene in Book VIII of *The Aeneid,* he comments about Venus, "ce que j'y trouve à considerer, c'est qu'il la peinct un peu bien esmeue pour une Venus maritale. En ce sage marché, les appetits ne se trouvent pas si follastres; ils sont sombres et plus mousses." [32] We have already discussed Montaigne's fear and avoidance of passion, so we may deduce that he needed to remove the passionate element from marriage in order to maintain the self-sufficiency so dear to his heart. With a wife who was essentially a comrade, he could be relatively comfortable; with a wife who exerted a powerful sexual hold, he would risk the loss of total control, both of the relationship and of himself. The alternative, then, was a limited sexual life.

---

[27] Montaigne, T. I, L. I, p. 227.
[28] *Ibid.,* T. II, L. III, p. 273.
[29] *Ibid.,* p. 327.
[30] *Ibid.,* T. I, L. I, pp. 200-201.
[31] *Ibid.,* T. II, L. III, p. 416.
[32] *Ibid.,* p. 273.

The lengthy digression on marriage that immediately follows the quotation from Virgil illustrates Montaigne's point: "Je ne vois point de mariages qui faillent plustost et se troublent que ceux qui s'acheminent par la beauté et desirs amoureux. Il y faut des fondemens plus solides et plus constans." [33] Although this view is an intelligent and valid one, its context is not as sound. An attentive reading of the *Essais* leads us to his conclusion that a good marriage is tantamount to friendship: "Ung bon mariage, s'il en est, refuse la compaignie et conditions de l'amour. Il tache à representer celles de l'amitié." [34] However, his idea of marital friendship is not exactly based on equality or even mutual respect; it is a far cry from his relationship with La Boétie. While he retains the freedom to travel and spend most of his time in the pleasurable pursuit of self-expression, "la plus utile et honnorable science et occupation à une femme, c'est la science du mesnage." [35] The implications of this statement are not as simple as they appear. The typical feminist reaction would be an angry one, and rightfully so. But we must understand that while reducing the woman to the role of a housewife, he also endows her with complete control of the home. He, in turn, becomes quite dependent on the wife since she literally runs the house; and this dependence constitutes the ultimate chain binding her to her role. He says in "De la vanité," "je me destourne volontiers du gouvernement de ma maison." [36]

Paul Laumonier makes us aware of the fine house-keeping virtues of Mme de Montaigne, which compensated for the economic nonchalance of her husband. [37] As Montaigne admits, "je me suis pris tard au mesnage ... toutefois, de ce que j'en ay veu, c'est un'occupation plus empeschante que difficile. ... Je m'y employe, mais despiteusement." [38] His words suggest little choice for Mrs. Montaigne; with a husband like hers, she had to have a great talent for management. In making the house her domain, Montaigne, like so many other husbands, limited the scope of her activity and pos-

---

[33] *Ibid.*, p. 273.
[34] *Ibid.*, T. II, L. II, p. 275.
[35] *Ibid.*, T. II, L. III, p. 415.
[36] *Ibid.*, p. 384.
[37] Paul Laumonier, "Madame de Montaigne d'après les *Essais*," *Mélanges offerts à M. Abel Lefranc* (Paris: Librairie E. Droz, n.d.), p. 393.
[38] Montaigne, T. II, L. III, p. 385.

sibility so that she could accommodate his desire for untroubled privacy. If she held the fort, so to speak, he could indulge in his love of travel.

In this respect Montaigne proves to be a master at defending himself. Of his frequent absences, he claims:

> Quant aux devoirs de l'amitié maritale qu'on pense estre interessez par cette absence, je ne le crois pas. ... Ces interruptions me remplissent d'une amour recente envers les miens et me redonnent l'usage de ma maison plus doux. [39]

Absence makes the heart grow fonder, indeed, but it appears that Montaigne's "amie maritale" was never given the same opportunity to arrive at that conclusion (nor were other women of the Renaissance). He writes laughingly that, in order to succeed, a marriage should unite a blind wife and a deaf husband. [40] And, as he mentions later, "il est toujours proclive aux femmes de disconvenir à leurs maris: elles saisissent à deux mains toutes couvertures de leur contraster; la première excuse leur sert de planiere justification." [41]

Much that Montaigne says of marriage is general, and discussion of his wife or his domestic life is limited. As a matter of fact, it is rather strange that a man who constantly analyzes himself devotes so little space to his existence as husband and father. Although Laumonier suggests that Montaigne "a eu le tact de ne pas nous parler de sa femme," [42] one might conclude that these roles were of little importance to him, and that domestic felicity did not figure greatly in his life. In fact, some of the passages suggest that not all was harmonious in his conjugal relationship; he throws a most revealing hint on the subject in the chapter "De la colere":

> J'advertis ceux qui ont loy de se pouvoir courroucer en ma famille: premierement, qu'ils mesnagent leur cholere et ne l'espandent pas à tout pris; car cela en empesche l'effect et le poix; la criaillerie temeraire et ordinaire passe en usage et faict que chacun la mesprise ... [43]

---

[39] *Ibid.*, pp. 415-416.
[40] *Ibid.*, p. 298.
[41] *Ibid.*, T. I, L. II, p. 433.
[42] Laumonier, pp. 394-395.
[43] Montaigne, T. II, L. II, pp. 124-125.

MONTAIGNE'S PERSONAL BACKGROUND AND WOMEN 51

In addition, the following comment seems like the result of a daily relationship with a stubborn woman:

> J'ay cogneu cent et cent femmes, car ils disent que les testes de Gascongne ont quelque prerogative en cela, que vous eussiez plustost faict mordre dans le fer chaut que de leur faire desmordre une opinion qu'elles eussent conçeue en cholere. [44]

Edith Sichel suggests that "Madame de Montaigne was probably something of a scold, and was undeterred by her husband's formidable speechlessness." [45] Montaigne obviously did not allow his wife to get the better of him; he could ignore her by taking a trip, or as was more often the case, locking himself in his private study.

He explains in "De la solitude" that "il faut avoir femmes, enfans ... mais non pas s'y attacher en manière que nostre heur en despende. Il se faut reserver une arriere boutique toute nostre, toute franche, en laquelle nous establissons nostre vraye liberté et principale retraicte et solitude." [46] If there is one thing Montaigne valued, it was his privacy, his ability to delve into himself, oblivious to external exigencies. He tells us in the chapter entitled "De trois commerces" about the tower he built on the side of his house, a retreat where he spent most of his time:

> Je passe là et la plus part des jours de ma vie, et la plus part des heures du jour. ... C'est là mon siege. J'essaie à m'en rendre la domination pure, et à soustraire ce seul coin à la communauté et conjugale, et filiale, et civile. ... Miserable à mon gré, qui n'a chez soy où estre à soy, où se faire particulièrement la cour, où se cacher! [47]

This tower represented essential liberty for Montaigne. Nobody was allowed to enter his tower, least of all his wife. Upon closing his door, in the subtle battle between the demands of the woman and the demands of the self, he could give total dominance to the latter.

---

[44] *Ibid.*, p. 131.
[45] Edith Sichel, *Michel de Montaigne* (London, 1911), p. 39.
[46] Montaigne, T. I, L. I, p. 271.
[47] *Ibid.*, T. II, L. III, p. 249.

Sainte-Beuve stresses that Montaigne "est retiré vers l'âge de trente-huit ans dans son château et dans sa tour seigneuriale." [48] It is most interesting to note that since he married at thirty-three years of age, he was anxious for solitude after only five years of marriage. This is partially due to the fact that habits can be well-formed by the age of thirty-three: he had lived up to that time in relative privacy, and the existence of a family, requiring certain responsibilities and compromises on his part, could have seemed like an intrusion. He admits, "j'ay une ame toute sienne, accoustumée à se conduire à sa mode. N'ayant eu jusques à cett'heure ny commandant ny maistre forcé, j'ay marché aussi avant et le pas qu'il m'a pleu. Cela m'a amolli et rendu inutile au service d'autruy, et ne m'a faict bon qu'à moy." [49] We may say that Montaigne gave his wife control over the home, not so much because it is inherent in the woman to manage the household, but because he didn't care to do it. Who better than the wife could free him from petty details? As Paul Bonnefon reminds us, "cette femme ... prenant pour elle les soucis matériels, elle lui ménagea la retraite et le repos qui convenaient à sa nature d'observateur." [50] But Montaigne was not even satisfied by her work; he declares he would give everything for a son-in-law to take over:

> L'un de mes souhaits pour cette heure, ce seroit de trouver un gendre qui sçeut appaster commodéement mes vieux ans et les endormir, entre les mains de qui je deposasse en toute souveraineté la conduite et usage de mes biens ... [51]

The wife kept the affairs in order and was responsible for the children's education. Bonnefon suggests that "Montaigne ... voulut que ses propres enfants — il n'eut que des filles — fussent confiés à la direction de leur mère. N'était-ce pas là, en même temps, le plus direct des hommages au bon sens et aux qualités modestes de sa compagne?" [52] However, Montaigne himself negates this possibility with the following passage:

---

[48] C. A. Sainte-Beuve, *Nouveaux Lundis* (Paris, Calmann-Levy, n.d.), Tome II, p. 156.
[49] Montaigne, T. II, L. II, p. 44.
[50] Paul Bonnefon, *Montaigne et ses amis* (Genève, 1969), p. 233.
[51] Montaigne, T. II, L. III, p. 390.
[52] Bonnefon, p. 89.

> C'est raison de laisser l'administration des affaires aux meres, pendant que les enfans ne sont pas en l'aage ... pour en manier la charge; mais le pere les a bien mal nourris, s'il ne peut esperer qu'en cet aage là ils auront plus de sagesse et de suffisance que sa femme, *veu l'ordinaire foiblesse du sexe.* [53] (Italics mine.)

Once again, the education of children is entrusted to Mme de Montaigne less for her abilities than for his lack of paternal feeling. Only one of his daughters, Leonor, survived; but when he was asked how many children he had, he could not remember.[54] In "De la vanité," he admits,

> Aussi n'ay-je poinct cette forte liaison qu'on dict attacher les hommes à l'advenir par les enfans qui portent leur nom et leur honneur, et en doibs desirer à l'avanture d'autant moins, s'ils sont si desirables. Je ne tiens que trop au monde et à cette vie par moy-mesme ... et n'ay jamais estimé qu'estre sans enfans fut un defaut qui deut rendre la vie moins complete et moins contente. La vacation sterile a bien aussi ses commoditez. Les enfans sont du nombre des choses qui n'ont pas fort dequoy estre desirées ... [55]

Indeed, Montaigne did not take much interest in his daughter. As Sichel so justly remarks,

> he seemed too intellectual to be a father — too intellectual and too lazy, for he could make no effort over his natural inclinations. Perhaps, too, he had too poor an idea of woman to draw much out of a daughter. Indulgent contempt does not make a very fruitful atmosphere, and it was with indulgent contempt that Montaigne surrounded his womankind. This, not confidence, was the motive which prompted him to leave Leonor's upbringing to her mother.[56]

But on the other hand, perhaps we can justify, to a certain extent, Montaigne's attitude towards children by noting that it may have been necessary for him to develop a certain insensitivity:

---

[53] Montaigne, T. I, L. II, p. 436.
[54] Frame, p. 94.
[55] Montaigne, T. II, L. III, p. 443.
[56] Sichel, pp. 42-43.

Montaigne and his wife had six daughters between 1570 and 1583, and five of them died before they reached six months of age.[57] Had he allowed himself the development of a strong attachment to his girls, the pain would have been extreme. Montaigne warned us earlier not to become so attached to people or things that they control our happiness; this would be especially true of children who had little chance of remaining alive. As he says of his private hideaway, "discourir et y rire comme sans femme, sans enfans ... afin que, quand l'occasion adviendra de leur perte, il ne nous soit pas nouveau de nous en passer."[58]

He did not let his feelings for any person, save La Boétie, dominate him, and was quite proud that he was not subject to the vile passion of jealousy: "Cette passion ... n'a de sa grace aucune addresse en moy."[59] Jealousy belongs rather to the world of women, and he is quick to condemn them for it:

> Lorsque la jalousie saisit ces pauvres ames foibles et sans resistance, c'est pitié comme elle les tirasse et tyrannise cruellement. ... La vertu, la santé, le merite, la reputation du mary sont les boutefeus de leur maltalent et de leur rage. ... Cette fiévre laidit et corrompt tout ce qu'elles ont de bel et de bon d'ailleurs, et d'une femme jalouse, quelque chaste qu'elle soit et mesnagere, il n'est action qui ne sente à l'aigre et à l'importun.[60]

He makes a great case of jealousy, perhaps because it can exist only as a function of strong attachment. He kills two birds with one stone, so to speak, for in passing judgment on one emotion, he implies condemnation of that other emotion from which it stems. He takes it a bit far when he applies Terence to the female complaint:

> Uxor, si cesses, aut te amare cogitat,
> Aut tete amari, aut potare, aut animo obsequi
> Et tibi bene esse soli, cum sibi sit malè.[61]

---

[57] Frame, p. 94.
[58] Montaigne, T. I, L. I, p. 271.
[59] *Ibid.*, T. II, L. III, p. 289.
[60] *Ibid.*, p. 291.
[61] *Ibid.*, p. 417. ("If you are late, your wife assumes you're having an affair with someone, or someone with you, drinking, banishing care; that

In light of his numerous references to jealousy and cuckoldry, it may be worthwhile to note a personal event of May, 1569. Montaigne tells us in the *Essais* that his third brother Armand, "le Capitaine S. Martin, aagé de vint et trois ans ... jouant à la paume, receut un coup d'esteuf. ... Cinq ou six heures après il mourut d'une Apoplexie que ce coup luy causa." [62] A rather peculiar affair was settled the same day. Frame tells us that Michel had discovered in his wife's coffers a gold chain that the deceased Armand de Montaigne had left there. Michel told this to his mother who declared that the chain belonged to her; so he returned it to her in the presence of his two brothers. [63]

The fact that Saint-Martin's chain was found in his sister-in-law's coffer raises a few questions. Some critics, such as Maurice Rat and Alexandre Nicolai, see in this episode the proof of adultery between Saint-Martin and Françoise.

Frame goes on to suggest that Françoise, who was a beautiful and lusty woman, was probably reacting to Montaigne's austere notion of marriage, so she "found consolation for her vexation by abandoning herself, a few months after the wedding, to Captain Saint-Martin ... who was young and handsome and did not hesitate, finding the opportunity convenient and his sister-in-law pleasing, to show her that she was attractive and to teach her immodesty." [64]

The essay on the shoe of Fabius in Book Three also focuses on infidelity; Montaigne alludes to an anecdote narrated by Plutarch in the "Vie de Paul Emile." Here, Montaigne takes his inspiration from a Roman who, when blamed for having repudiated his lovely wife, answered that his new shoe, though fine-looking, hurt his foot: "Joinct le soulier neuf et bien formé ... qui vous blesse le pied; et que l'estranger n'entend pas combien il vous couste et combien vous prestez à maintenir l'apparence de cet ordre qu'on voit en vostre famille, et qu'à l'avanture l'achetez vous trop cher." [65] It is possible that Montaigne's shoe pinched as much as the one of

---

you alone have all the fun, she all the ills to bear." *Complete Works...*, p. 746.)

[62] *Ibid.*, T. I, L. I, p. 86.
[63] Frame, p. 26.
[64] *Ibid.*, p. 90.
[65] Montaigne, T. II, L. III, p. 385.

Fabius. We must admit, of course, that no substantial proof exists for this possibility.

Even if adultery was the case, Montaigne may not have been terribly bothered about it in any event. Besides his declaration of freedom from jealousy, he takes up a good deal of space treating cuckoldry in a rather light manner. He claims,

> chacun de vous a faict quelqu'un coqu: or nature est toute en pareilles, en compensation et vicissitude. La frequence de cet accident en doibt meshuy avoir moderé l'aigreur; le voilà tantost passé en coustume. [66]

Whether this remark is general or particular is impossible to ascertain, but is seems a bit more specific when he says, "je sçay çant honestes hommes coqus, honnestement et peu indecemment. Un galant homme en est pleint, non pas desestimé." [67] He even remarks, "j'en sçay qui à leur escient ont tiré et proffit et avancement du cocuage, dequoy le seul nom effraye tant de gens." [68] In any case, we shall never know whether the basis for his discussion of cuckoldry was experiential, for despite his frankness, "la coustume rende indecent et nuisible qu'on communique à personne tout ce qu'on en sçait et qu'on en sent." [69]

It would be a mistake to assume that Montaigne had nothing good to say to or about his wife. We should remember that he dedicated La Boétie's translation of Plutarch's "Consolatio ad Uxorem" (*Plutarch's Moralia,* The Loeb Classical Library, 1959) to her. But once again, this act has many complexities beneath its surface: it took place in 1570, following the death of their first child. Witnessing his wife's sorrow, Montaigne left to Plutarch the duty of consoling her. His letter to her is less a loving dedication than a reminder of her duties:

> Ma femme, vous entendez bien que ce n'est pas le tour d'un galant homme ... de vous courtiser et caresser encores: car ils disent qu'un habile homme peult bien prendre femme; mais que de l'espouser c'est à faire à un sot.

---

[66] *Ibid.,* p. 297.
[67] *Ibid.,* p. 296.
[68] *Ibid.,* T. I, L. I, p. 61.
[69] *Ibid.,* T. II, L. III, p. 297.

> Laissons les dire: je me tiens, de ma part, à la simple façon du vieil aage. ... Vivons, ma femme, vous et moy, à la vieille françoise. ... Mais je laisse à Plutarque la charge de vous consoler, et de vous advertir de vostre debvoir en cela, vous priant le croire pour l'amour de moy; car il vous descouvrira mes intentions ... beaucoup mieulx que je ne ferois moy mesme. [70]

It seems that for any affection he showed her, he immediately qualified or even negated it. This occurs most glaringly in the famous incident of the horse: the first thing he does when he regains consciousness after a fall is to order a horse for his wife, "que je voyoy s'empestrer et se tracasser dans le chemin, qui est montueux et mal-aisé." [71] But instead of leaving this considerate gesture alone, he adds afterwards, "cette consideration ... des pensemens vains ... ne venoyent pas de chez moy." [72] He makes it appear that concern for his wife is a mechanical rather than affective thing.

It is interesting to note that this man who was so condescending to his wife was extremely gallant when he addressed himself publicly to great ladies. These two contradictory forms of behavior go together quite well. It is finally not at all inconsistent for a man to place women on pedestals when they are at a distance, and treat them poorly in private; it is simply a version of that familiar dichotomy between public appearance and private reality, between the word and the deed (a dichotomy especially popular with writers). He sings praises to the self-sacrifice of the "Trois bonnes femmes" of Pliny the Younger, Cecinna Paetus and Seneca, respectively, each of whom "abandonna ... sa vie pour le repos de celle de son mary"; [73] but the bulk of his personal testimony speaks against sacrifice, urging us to live for ourselves rather than for others. Perhaps we are to understand that men should live for themselves, even though women should live for their men.

His dedication to Madame de Duras at the end of "De la ressemblance des enfans aux peres" treats the very problem of the distance between words and experience. He comments upon writers

---

[70] Montaigne, "A Madamoiselle de Montaigne, ma femme," T. II, p. 611.
[71] *Ibid.*, T. I, L. II, p. 413.
[72] *Ibid.*, p. 413.
[73] *Ibid.*, T. II, L. II, p. 154.

whose lives do not reflect their fine books: "Ceux que je voy faire des bons livres sous des mechantes chausses, eussent premierement faict leurs chausses, s'ils m'en eussent creu."[74] He rebels against the possibility that he could be among them: "Mon Dieu! Madame, que je haïrois une telle recommandation d'estre habile homme par escrit, et estre un homme de neant et un sot ailleurs."[75] Yet, there is an undeniable distance between his verbal flattery and domestic behavior when it comes to women.

When he dedicates the essay "De l'institution des enfans" to Madame Diane de Foix, Comtesse de Gurson,[76] or "Vingt et neuf sonnets d'Estienne de La Boetie" to Madame de Grammont, Comtesse de Guissen, his flattery is equivalent to a literary convention:

> Il est peu de dames en France qui jugent mieux et se servent plus à propos que vous de la poësie; et puis, qu'il n'en est point qui la puissent rendre vive et animée, comme vous faites par ces beaux et riches accords dequoy, parmy un million d'autres beautez, nature vous a estrenée.[77]

He then dedicates "De l'affection des peres aux enfans" to Madame d'Estissac,[78] and in "De l'yvrongnerie" he speaks of "une dame que j'honnore et prise singulierement"[79] who is Madame d'Aimar, wife of the president of the Parliament of Bordeaux. It is obvious that Montaigne enjoys paying homage, or lip service, to beautiful and distinguished ladies, while his personal life is characterized by a more selfish and condescending attitude towards his wife.

---

[74] *Ibid.*, p. 200.
[75] *Ibid.*, pp. 200-201.
[76] *Ibid.*, T. I, L. I, p. 154.
[77] *Ibid.*, p. 212.
[78] *Ibid.*, p. 422.
[79] *Ibid.*, p. 375.

CHAPTER V

MONTAIGNE AND MARIE DE GOURNAY

Her role in the history of feminism

A close reading of the *Essais* gives evidence of a subtle progression in Montaigne's discussion of women. Early in the work, his comments are predominantly negative and he sprinkles every few pages with anecdotes that mock women. For example, he declares, "si on les occupe à certain sujet, qui les bride et contreigne, ils se jettent desreiglez, par-cy par là, dans le vague champ des imaginations."[1] But towards the end of the *Essais,* he makes exceptions to his severity regarding women and seems to acquire the ability to see their more positive aspects. Since this shift occurred at approximately the same time that he met Marie de Gournay, we may find it worthwhile to study her close relationships with both Montaigne and feminism.

When they met in Paris, Montaigne was about fifty-five; Marie de Gournay was only twenty-three. The close friendship that ensued produced the third edition of the *Essais* (1595); it may be said that we owe this posthumous edition to her devotion to Montaigne.[2] Their first encounter was the result of Marie's admiration for the *Essais*: she wrote to him when he arrived in Paris and he, in turn, went to see her. Their mutual enthusiasm was immediate: he adopted her as his "fille d'alliance" and she began her lifelong devotion to his work. It was an alliance of souls, a platonic friend-

---

[1] Montaigne, T. I, L. I, p. 29.
[2] Lester G. Crocker, *The Selected Essays of Montaigne* (New York, 1959), pp. xii-xiii.

ship that centered on literature. Their relationship was mainly epistolary, but at one time he stayed at her home (the Château de Gournay in Picardy) for three months. According to Estienne Pasquier, "il sejourna trois mois en deux voyages, avec tous les honnestes accueils que l'on pourroit souhaitter." [3]

Marjorie Ilsley informs us that Marie was "a highly emotional girl ... capable of great enthusiasm, of complete devotion to people and causes" [4] and we find that the objects of her energy were Montaigne and the feminist movement. Indeed, we can sense Marie's spontaneous admiration for the *Essais* and their author from the manner in which she consecrated herself to increasing his fame. Her efforts on behalf of his popularity were rivalled only by her commitment to women's rights.

Bonnefon remarks that her intelligence rendered her so different from her contemporaries that she did not belong to her epoch. [5] We learn that she studied without the aid of teachers, owing to the antagonism of her mother who "aportoit de l'aversion au goût très vif de sa fille pour l'étude." [6] She also set herself apart from other women in that she was an ardent advocate of women's rights. Richardson calls her "one of the staunchest defenders of the right of her sex that her country produced." [7]

Marie's originality lies in the manner in which she opposed the injustices of men against women. She expounds her theories in *Egalité des hommes et des femmes* (1622):

> La pluspart de ceux qui prennent la cause des femmes, contre cette orgueilleuse preferance que les hommes s'attribuent, leur rendent le change entier; r'envoyans la preferance vers elles. Moy qui fuys toutes extremitez, je me contente de les esgaler aux hommes. [8]

---

[3] Estienne Pasquier, *Choix de lettres sur la littérature, la langue et la traduction* (Genève, 1956), p. 49.

[4] Marjorie Ilsley, *A Daughter of the Renaissance: Marie le Jars de Gournay* (The Hague, 1963), p. 17.

[5] Bonnefon, p. 315.

[6] Mario Schiff, *La Fille d'alliance de Montaigne, Marie de Gournay* (Paris, 1910), p. 2.

[7] Richardson, p. 154.

[8] Marie de Gournay, "Egalité des hommes et des femmes" in Schiff, p. 61.

She proceeds by asserting that nature is opposed to either sex claiming inferiority or superiority to the other. According to her thesis, man and woman are simply two equal human beings: "L'homme et la femme sont tellement uns, que si l'homme est plus que la femme, la femme est plus que l'homme." [9] In her desire to accord to women the benefits of equality, Marie gives evidence of independence of judgment. Certain contemporary feminists pursue her line of thought in the sense that they do not wish to work against men, but rather to collaborate with them. The basis for this view is that feminine qualities complement masculine ones, and that both are necessary.

Marie turns to predecessors and contemporaries, choosing Erasmus, Agrippa and Castiglione ("cet honneste et pertinent Precepteur des courtisans" [10]) as examples of men who were sympathetic to the female cause. In addition, she alludes to the authority of God and the Bible to make her point: "Jesus-Christ est appellé fils de l'homme bien qu'il ne le soit que de la femme." [11]

One of her main targets is the discrepancy between the kinds of education given to boys and to girls. She feels that it is the inequality of intellectual development, rather than the inferiority of the female sex, that breeds further inequality:

> Que si les dames arrivent moins souvent que les hommes, aux degrez d'excellence, c'est merveille que le deffaut de bonne instruction, voire l'affluence de la mauvaise expresse et professoire ne face pis, les gardant d'y pouvoir arriver du tout. Se trouve til plus de difference des hommes à elles que d'elles à elles mesmes, selon l'institution qu'elles ont prinse, selon qu'elles son eslevées en ville ou village, ou selon les Nations? [12]

Her primary goal is equal instruction for everyone of both sexes, the educational equality achieved by modern feminists a long time ago.

In her discussion of major thinkers favorable to her cause, she manages to include Plutarch ("au Traicté des vertueux faicts des

---

[9] *Ibid.*, p. 70.
[10] *Ibid.*, p. 67.
[11] *Ibid.*, p. 70.
[12] *Ibid.*, p. 65.

femmes maintient; que la vertu de l'homme et de la femme est mesme chose" [13]) and Seneca (" ... la Nature n'a point traicté les dames ingratement ... mais qu'elle les a doüées de pareille vigueur et de pareille faculté à toute chose honeste et louable" [14]), and does not fail to mention Montaigne. She remarks,

> Voyons, ce qu'en juge apres ceux deux, le tiers chef du Triumvirat de la sagesse humaine et morale en ses Essais. Il luy semble, dit-il, et si ne sçait pourquoy, qu'il se trouve rarement des femmes dignes de commander aux hommes. ... Il craint d'avoir tort. ... N'oubliant pas au reste d'alleguer et relever en autre lieu de son mesme livre, cette authorité que Platon leur depart en sa Republique ... [15]

We can see that she is already aware of Montaigne's contradictory opinions regarding women. Later, she focuses on another problem and her attack contains the germ of the political claims of modern feminists. She takes a stand against "la loy Salique, qui prive les femmes de la couronne," [16] and adds that this law is applied only in France. Montaigne's attitude in this matter is as follows:

> Il est dangereux de laisser à leur jugement la dispensation de nostre succession, ... car cet appetit desreglé et goust malade qu'elles ont au temps de leurs groisses, elles l'ont en l'ame en tout temps. [17]

This comment represents the ultimate antifeminist position: an attack which seems to constitute fear of a loss of male authority. Marie may have felt an obligation to show that Montaigne was wrong and, in point of fact, her intelligence did prove that his generalization was unfair.

Marie de Gournay's forceful personality is again evident in her *Grief des dames* (1625) in which she makes known her indignation at the status of women and at their limited possibilities: "Bienheureus es-tu lecteur, si tu n'es point de ce sexe, qu'on interdict

---

[13] *Ibid.*, p. 66.
[14] *Ibid.*, p. 66.
[15] *Ibid.*, pp. 66-67.
[16] *Ibid.*, p. 68.
[17] Montaigne, T. I, L. II, p. 438.

de tous les biens, l'interdisant de la liberté."[18] She takes the side of literate women who had to suffer because of men's simultaneous refusal to take them seriously and their insistence upon domination. Marie, too, had a difficult time in establishing herself as a woman writer, for the "femme savante" was not yet appreciated by society. As Montaigne puts it, " ... une fame estoit assez sçavante quand elle sçavoit mettre difference entre la chemise et le pourpoint de son mary."[19] Montaigne appears not to have believed in women's influence in the intellectual development of men. This was precisely the point of view that enraged Marie. She declares angrily that some men refuse even to read works published by women: "J'en ay cogneu qui mesprisoient absolument les Oeuvres des femmes, sans se daigner amuser à les lire pour sçavoir de quelle estoffe elles sont."[20]

Though opposed to the oppression of women, she remains tactful and is careful not to condemn men unjustly: she defends women without "donner a priori l'avantage à l'un ni à l'autre ..."[21] Her intelligence and articulateness lead Abensour to call her "l'initiatrice, après Christine de Pisan, du féminisme moderne."[22] The *Egalité des hommes et des femmes* offers us a clear picture of the evolution that feminism underwent at the end of the sixteenth century. As far as her impact on the future course of the women's movement is concerned, critics ascribe to her a major role in the development of feminist ideas. Ilsley explains that Marie "persistently defied the custom of her time in order to preserve her right to live a life free from the shackles of old conventions, a life devoted to the calling of her choice. She thus became one of the rare professional women writers of her time, espousing causes that were judged inappropriate for women to defend."[23] Her work as Montaigne's editor was in itself an important step in the feminist direction for, at a time when her sex was confined to the home, she established herself as one of the first women editors. We owe much of the credit for Montaigne's reputation and popularity to her defense of

---

[18] Marie de Gournay, "Grief des dames" in Schiff, p. 89.
[19] Montaigne, T. I, L. I, p. 150.
[20] Schiff, p. 94.
[21] *Ibid.*, p. 48.
[22] Abensour, p. ix.
[23] Ilsley, p. 279.

the *Essais* and to the eleven editions brought out under her editorship.[24]

Her influence on Montaigne

But what was Montaigne's position on the question of educated women? We find passages in the *Essais* where he opposes the notion of the woman as scholar:

> Que leur faut-il, que vivre aymées et honnorées? Elles n'ont et ne sçavent que trop pour cela. ... Quand je les voy attachées à la rhetorique, à la judiciaire, à la logique et semblables drogueries si vaines et inutiles à leur besoing, j'entre en crainte que les hommes qui le leur conseillent, le facent pour avoir loy de les regenter soubs ce tiltre. Car quelle autre excuse leur trouverois-je? ... Si toutefois il leur fache de nous ceder en quoy que ce soit, et veulent par curiosité avoir part aux livres, la poësie est un amusement propre à leur besoin; c'est un art follastre et subtil, desguisé, parlier, tout en plaisir, tout en montre comme elles.[25]

We are left, therefore, with his denigration of women on the one hand, and the contrary testimony of his relationship with Marie de Gournay on the other. It is in keeping with Montaigne's paradoxical nature that the closest friend of his later years was an ardent feminist. But it is hard to believe that this young woman whom Bonnefon describes as "guère femme à se constraindre. Elle préféra batailler inutilment, presque seule contre tous, que transiger ou déposer les armes,"[26] upset Montaigne's earlier thoughts about the female sex. If we go back to Book I, he explains that, as far as friendship is concerned,

> ... la suffisance ordinaire des femmes n'est pas pour respondre à cette conference et communication, nourisse de cette saincte couture; ny leur ame ne semble assez ferme pour soustenir l'estreinte d'un noeud si pressé et si durable. ... Ce sexe par nul exemple n'y est encore peu arriver.[27]

How, then, did Marie change his mind?

---

[24] *Ibid.*, p. 279.
[25] Montaigne, T. II, L. III, pp. 242-243.
[26] Bonnefon, p. 316.
[27] Montaigne, T. I, L. I, pp. 201-202.

After the death of La Boétie, Montaigne often longed for the kind of friendship they had shared; we know from his comments about his wife that she possessed neither the intellectual nor the spiritual qualities displayed by La Boétie. Then Montaigne finds Marie de Gournay, an unusually bright young woman who sees an affinity between Montaigne's mind and her own. It is possible that his initial response was to feel flattered by her admiration; Bonnefon suggests that

> Montaigne éprouva une grande joie à se voir ainsi compris et admiré; cet enthousiasme si sincère lui réchauffa le cœur. Il semble qu'il se crut plus sûr de l'avenir, maintenant qu'une jeune piété filiale veillerait sur sa mémoire. [28]

Another possibility is that there was a strong element of paternal love in the adoption of Marie as his "fille d'alliance." As we learned in the previous chapter, he lost a total of five daughters. Bonnefon agrees that "celle qui devait être plus tard la fille d'alliance de Montaigne eût pu parfaitement être sa fille selon la nature, car c'est le temps ... elle était donc née le 6 octobre 1565 ... où le philosophe prenait femme et épousait Françoise de la Chassaigne." [29]

But the most likely basis for their "alliance" appears to be a shared intellectual curiosity and capacity. In her Preface to the 1595 edition of the *Essais*, we see the extent to which she felt her thought patterns resembled those of Montaigne:

> ... le seul contentement que i'euz oncques de moy-mesme, c'est d'auoir rencontré plusieurs choses parmy les dernieres additions que tu [le lecteur] verras en ce volume, lesquelles i'auois imaginées toutes pareilles, auant que les auoir veues. [30]

Many of their ideas were similar; Ilsley tells us that "Montaigne soon found that this young woman agreed with him upon the superiority of friendship over love." [31] On the other hand, being

---

[28] Bonnefon, p. 157.
[29] *Ibid.*, p. 317.
[30] "Preface" in *Essais de Michel Seignevr de Montaigne* (Paris, 1595), [pp. xiii-xiv].
[31] Ilsley, p. 27.

a woman, she did not share his appreciation of marriage, and was less sensitive to material than spiritual matters. As the *Essais* informed us, the marriage of the time limited the woman to being a mother and housewife, absorbed by the manual work for her husband and children: "Tout porte à croire que les liens normaux entre maris et femmes étaient surtout d'ordre matériel." [32]

Marie de Gournay did express ideas about marriage that were rather unusual for her time. Pasquier explains that "la Damoiselle de Jars ... ne s'est proposé d'avoir jamais autre mary que son honneur, enrichi par la lecture des bons livres; & sur tous les autres, des *Essais* du Seigneur de Montaigne." [33] And Ilsley maintains that Marie "disapproved of the customary 'mariage de convenance' and would have accepted only a union based on mutual affection. She preferred friendship ennobled by spiritual love to marriage without it." [34]

Marie was obviously more interested in learning than in marriage; in a manner similar to that of Montaigne, she avoided the practical responsibilities of everyday existence and escaped into her own world of books. The *Essais* became her constant companion and she felt that she knew Montaigne well even before she met him.

Once they got to know each other, Montaigne was again able to taste the sweetness of friendship, "une chaleur constante et rassize, toute douceur et polissure." [35] He finally found an intelligent companion with whom he could share his philosophical sensibility, as he had done with La Boétie. Bonnefon mentions that he "établissait sans doute dans son esprit quelque comparison entre ces deux amitiés dont l'une avait fait la joie de ses premières années et dont l'autre devait faire la consolation des dernières." [36] Montaigne proves eloquent in his praise of Marie towards the end of Book II:

> J'ay pris plaisir à publier en plusieurs lieux l'esperance que j'ay de Marie de Gournay le Jars, ma fille d'alliance,

---

[32] Marie de Gournay, *Les Idées littéraires de Mlle de Gournay*, ed. Anne Uildriks (Groningen, 1926), p. 23.
[33] Pasquier, p. 49.
[34] Ilsley, p. 35.
[35] Montaigne, T. I, L. I, p. 201.
[36] Bonnefon, p. 320.

> et certes aymée de moy beaucoup plus que paternellement, et enveloppée en ma retraitte et solitude, comme l'une des meilleures parties de mon propre estre. Je ne regarde plus qu'elle au monde. Si l'adolescence peut donner presage, cette ame sera quelque jour capable des plus belles choses, et entre autres de la perfection de cette trèssaincte amitié où nous ne lisons point que son sexe ait peu monter encores. La sinceritéet la solidité de ses meurs y sont desjà bastantes, son affection vers moy plus que sur-abondante, et telle en somme qu'il n'y a rien à souhaiter ... [37]

The extent of his admiration for her can be inferred from the fact that he wrote "je ne regarde plus qu'elle au monde" while his wife and daughter were alive. In addition, we should remember the nature of his relationship with Françoise, as well as his opinion that women should be confined to household affairs.

Edith Sichel makes an important point about Montaigne's relationship to women:

> After all, if Montaigne's marriage was not ideal, it was not entirely his fault. Had he known nobler or more intelligent women, his standard would probably have altered. His friendship at the end of his life with the intellectual Mademoiselle de Gournay, his fille d'alliance, although it involved the flattery of a young girl's adulation of a great man already growing old, was not devoid of significance. [38]

Her remark is supported by Montaigne's discussion "De l'amitié" where he explains that the kind of union of souls that he considers friendship is possible only between persons of intelligence. [39]

A question may arise as to the existence of any physical attraction between them, especially if we remember from Chapter II how Montaigne appreciated the sight of beautiful women. However, Montaigne appears to have been drawn to Marie for any reason save physical. We learn from Thérèse Casevitz that Marie

> ... n'était pas jolie. Sur le portrait, mis par elle en tête de l'édition de 1641 des 'Advis ou presents' ... représentée à l'age de trente-et-un ans, nous la voyons, coiffée avec

---
[37] Montaigne, T. II, L. II, p. 66.
[38] Sichel, p. 45.
[39] Montaigne, T. I, L. I, pp. 203-204.

coquetterie, la chevelure surmontée d'un long voile, le regard intelligent, mais le nez pointu, les lèvres pincées, au total sans beauté et sans grâce.[40]

Other critics concur with this view of Marie's appearance: Ilsley states that "she was often labelled a homely woman and jokes were made about her physical unattractiveness,"[41] and l'abbé de Marolles declares that "sa beauté était plus de l'esprit que du corps."[42]

Marie was therefore a suitable companion for the essayist: she was seemingly devoid of the passionate attraction against which he was on guard, and capable of rising to his level, despite her sex. Montaigne must have realized that this young woman was an exception to his previous conception of womanhood. Their relationship proved to be quite an experience for him and he was not ashamed to admit it; he added to the *Essais* a passage

> fort louangeur pour Mlle de Gournay et vantait autant la justesse de son esprit que la bonté de son cœur. Les termes de cet éloge étaient si chaleureux que les malveillants en médirent. Cet outrage fut très sensible à Mlle de Gournay comme il l'eût été à Montaigne, s'il avait pu prévoir le langage des sots. Aussi la savante fille, autant par modestie que par crainte de la calomnie, effaça-t-elle ensuite des *Essais* tout ce qui lui sembla exagéré sur son propre mérite.[43]

They wrote to each other often but their letters have unfortunately been lost.[44] It almost seems suspicious that this correspondence, which would have provided the only evidence for the nature of their relationship, has disappeared. The only other literary remnant of their association (outside of the *Essais*) is given to us by Marie in the form of her novel, *Le Provmenoir de Monsieur de Montaigne* (1594). After they walked together in her château, she

---

[40] Thérèse Casevitz, "Mademoiselle de Gournay et le féminisme," *Revue Politique et Littéraire*, LXI (December, 1925), p. 769.

[41] Ilsley, p. 30.

[42] Michel de Marolles, *Mémoires de Michel de Marolles, abbé de Villeoin* (Amsterdam, 1755), I, p. 110.

[43] Bonnefon, p. 158.

[44] Anna Adele Chenot, "Marie de Gournay, Feminist and Friend of Montaigne," *Poet Lore*, XXXIV (January-December, 1923), p. 67.

remembered a subject from Plutarch's *Accidents of Love,* which they had read together. She decided to write a short novel for her "père d'alliance." According to Ilsley, "it was to become her first published work. This incident must have occurred ... during his last visit to Gournay-sur-Aronde. Unfortunately we know nothing further about Montaigne's long talks with Marie. Either she missed this unique opportunity to record the words of her literary father or the documents have been lost." [45]

The heroine of the novel is unmarried and wishes to escape a "mariage de convenance." Although the theme was not of Marie's invention, it gave her the opportunity to expose her ideas about marriage and to declare a woman's right to personal liberty. The letter preceding the text is dedicated to none other than "Michel Seigneur de Montaigne." Here she expresses her sentiments for him:

> Vous excuserez mon aage, et la bien-veillance que vous me portez, luy concedera son pardon, si la raison luy refuse. Certes si quelqu'un s'esbahit dequoi n'estans pere et fille que de tiltre, cette bienveillance la qui nous allie ensemble, surpasse neantmoins celle des vrays peres et enfans.... Il faut entrer aux amitiés par les portes de la vertu, qui veut estre biĕ asseuré de n'en sortir que par celles de la mort. [46]

Can we conclude that Marie de Gournay had an important influence on Montaigne's concepts of womanhood? Was she consulted while the second edition of the *Essais* was being prepared? Mario Schiff states that "deux additions des plus importantes ont été écrites sous sa dictée par Marie de Gournay et achevées ou corrigées ensuite par lui." [47] It is evident that Montaigne found in her a thirst for knowledge combined with deep comprehension, characteristics he never thought possible in a woman. In Book I, he declared of women,

> n'ayant point assez de force de discours pour choisir et embrasser ce qui le vaut, elles se laissent plus volontiers aller où les impressions de nature sont plus seules; comme

---

[45] Ilsley, p. 32.
[46] Marie de Gournay, *Le Provmenoir de monsieur de Montaigne. Par sa fille d'alliance* (Paris, 1594), p. 3.
[47] Schiff, p. 6.

> les animaux, qui n'ont cognoissance de leurs petits, que pendant qu'ils tiennent à leur mamelle.[48]

But could he speak the same way about the opposite sex after meeting Marie? Could a comment such as

> et ay par experience apperçeu que cette aigreur et aspreté de courage malitieux et inhumain s'accompaigne coustumierement de mollesse feminine,[49]

take account of qualities he appreciated in her? The fact that Marie as a woman proved capable of deep affection and lasting devotion must have convinced Montaigne that women could rise to the high ideal of friendship. As Ilsley puts it,

> Marie poured all her enthusiasm, her admiration, her love into this newly found friendship. Her emotions remained on a high spiritual level, her soul and mind alone involved. ... He ... found in Marie's freshness, her candor, her genius for rapid and profound understanding and her eagerness to learn, traits he had never expected to find in a woman.[50]

And Montaigne himself says of her,

> le jugement qu'elle fit des premiers *Essays,* et femme, et en ce siecle, et si jeune, et seule en son quartier, et la vehemence fameuse dont elle m'ayma et me desira long temps sur la seule estime qu'elle en print de moy, avant m'avoir veu, c'est un accident de très-digne consideration.[51]

There seems to be no question that the influence of Marie de Gournay was a positive one as far as Montaigne's treatment of women is concerned. Not only did she further the feminist cause through her writings, but her own sterling character strengthened the case for women since her life provided a clear example of the potential intelligence, commitment and high moral quality of women. We can sense her effect on Montaigne if we read the end of the chapter "Sur des vers de Virgile" while keeping in mind her con-

---

[48] Montaigne, T. I, L. II, pp. 438-439.
[49] *Ibid.,* T. II, L. II, p. 96.
[50] Ilsley, p. 31.
[51] Montaigne, T. II, L. II, p. 66.

victions in *Egalité des hommes et des femmes*; Montaigne alludes to Plato who approved of the participation of both men and women in "... tous estudes, exercices, charges, vacations guerrieres et paisibles, en sa republique,"[52] and to Antisthenes who "ostoit toute distinction entre leur vertu et la nostre."[53] It is apparent that this supremely intelligent feminist left her mark on Montaigne when he declares, "je dis que les masles et femelles sont jettez au mesme moule; sauf l'institution et l'usage, la difference n'y est pas grande."[54]

---

[52] *Ibid.*, T. II, L. III, p. 328.
[53] *Ibid.*, p. 328.
[54] *Ibid.*, p. 328.

Chapter VI

MONTAIGNE'S CONCEPTS OF WOMANHOOD

We have already witnessed two important aspects of Montaigne's treatment of women in the *Essais*: that it is often contradictory, and that part of it may be linked to his attempts to guard against the dangers of sexuality. Whether Montaigne can be labeled an anti-feminist or not is actually of little importance. It is only in exploring the reasons for one stance or another that we may reach a deeper level of understanding, both of Montaigne and of the roots of anti-feminism. Ironically enough, to place him in one category or another would be misleading for another reason: though we may conclude that he is an antifeminist by our own standards, many of the favorable things he says about women would qualify him for the title of feminist by sixteenth century standards.

For example, his primary expectations of a woman are that she be chaste and a good housewife. While these qualities may strike a modern woman as being unsatisfactory goals, we should remember that they were values of the time, held to be valid by women as well as men. And his depiction of the woman as childbearer,

> le plus ardu et le plus vigoureus des humains devoirs, nous l'avons resigné aux dames, et leur en quittons la gloire. Cela leur doit servir d'un singulier esguillon à s'y opiniastrer; c'est une belle matiere à nous braver et à fouler aux pieds cette vaine præminence de valeur et de vertu que nous pretendons sur elles,[1]

---

[1] Montaigne, T. II, L. III, p. 287.

though limiting her scope in life, is meant to be in her favor. Another problem posed is that while the modern woman wants to be admired for more than her physical attributes, Montaigne's appreciation of beauty constitutes a positive attitude: "C'est le vray avantage des dames que la beauté. Elle est si leur que la nostre, quoy qu'elle desire des traicts un peu autres, n'est en son point que confuse avec la leur, puerile et imberbe." [2] The distance between Montaigne's era and our own is perhaps best exemplified by his assertion that "c'est donc folie d'essayer à brider aux femmes un desir que leur est si cuysant et si naturel. Et, quand je les oy se vanter d'avoir leur volonté si vierge et si froide, je me moque d'elles; elles se reculent trop arriere." [3] Although one of the major complaints of today's feminists is that women are regarded primarily as sex objects, Montaigne's comment is basically pro-feminist, functioning as a defense of women's desire.

In fact, many passages in the *Essais* constitute a defense of women. He admits, "les femmes n'ont pas tort du tout quand elles refusent les reigles de vie qui sont introduites au monde, d'autant que ce sont les hommes qui les ont faictes sans elles." [4] He is able to see beyond the exclusively selfish male view, and sides with them against the men who boast of their conquests:

> A present les entretiens ordinaires des assemblées et des tables, ce sont les vanteries des faveurs receües et liberalité secrette des dames. Vrayement c'est trop d'abjection et de bassesse de cœur de laisser ainsi fierement persecuter, pestrir et fourrager ces tendres graces à des personnes ingrates, indiscrettes et si volages. [5]

For the infidelity of certain women, he puts more blame on men and their laws: comparing France and Italy, he concludes that the marriages of the latter "là clochent en cecy: leur coustume donne communement la loy si rude aus femmes, et si serve, que la plus esloignée accointance avec l'estranger leur est autant capitale que la plus voisine. Cette loy faict que toutes les approches se rendent

---

[2] *Ibid.*, p. 247.
[3] *Ibid.*, p. 293.
[4] *Ibid.*, p. 278.
[5] *Ibid.*, p. 289.

necessairement substantieles."⁶ In most of his discussions of women, he insists that women and lust are synonymous. The following statement, while a defense of women, renders them essentially sexual creatures:

> ...nous faisons et poisons les vices non selon nature, mais selon nostre interest, par où ils prennent tant de formes inegales. L'aspreté de nos decretz rend l'application des femmes à ce vice [lasciveté] plus aspre et vicieuse que ne porte sa condition, et l'engage à des suites pires que n'est leur cause.⁷

He also points out the hypocrisy of modesty: "Nous avons apris aux Dames de rougir oyant seulement nommer ce qu'elles ne craignent aucunement à faire."⁸ He admits that the very idea men form of their chastity is ridiculous, and adds sarcastically, "il faut qu'elles deviennent insensibles et invisibles pour nous satisfaire."⁹

Montaigne extends his defense of women into the realm of prostitution and once again sides with them against possessive males:

> ...d'où peut venir cette usurpation d'authorité souveraine que vous prenez sur celles qui vous favorisent à leurs despens?... que vous en investissez incontinent l'interest, la froideur et une auctorité maritale? C'est une convention libre: que ne vous y prenez vous comme vous les y voulez tenir? Il n'y a point de prescription sur les choses volontaires.¹⁰

In point of fact, the prostitute proves to be an extremely positive symbol for Montaigne, for she best fulfills his concept, "il faut se prester à autruy et ne se donner qu'à soy-mesme."¹¹ We find a paradox in his endorsement of chastity on the one hand and his respect for independence on the other: "Elles ne vendent que le

---

⁶ *Ibid.*, p. 312.
⁷ *Ibid.*, p. 287.
⁸ *Ibid.*, T. II, L. II, p. 31.
⁹ *Ibid.*, T. II, L. III, p. 294.
¹⁰ *Ibid.*, p. 319.
¹¹ *Ibid.*, p. 447.

corps; la volonté ne peut estre mise en vente, elle est trop libre et trop sienne." [12]

He pursues the subject of the intensity of female sexuality and comments on the inconstant and violent nature of love:

> Nous sommes, quasi en tout, iniques juges de leurs actions comme elles sont des nostres... mais si est-il vrai que c'est contre la nature de l'amour s'il n'est violant, et contre la nature de la violence s'il est constant. Et ceux qui s'en estonnent, s'en escrient et cerchent les causes de cette maladie en elles, comme desnaturée et incroyable, que ne voyent-ils combien souvent ils la reçoyvent en eux sans espouvantement et sans miracle! [13]

If we remember that Montaigne often struggles against passionate transports in his own life, we can find one of the possible reasons for the continuation of this discourse. For one who seeks tranquillity and avoids agitation, passion becomes a distinct problem:

> Ce n'est pas une passion simplement corporelle: si on ne trouve point de bout en l'avarice et en l'ambition, il n'y en a non plus en la paillardise. Elle vit encore après la satieté; et ne luy peut on prescrire ny satisfaction constante, ny fin; elle va tousjours outre sa possession. [14]

From this analysis, he concludes that fickleness is more pardonable in women than in men: "Elles peuvent alleguer comme nous l'inclination, qui nous est commune, à la varieté et à la nouvelleté, et alleguer secondement, sans nous, qu'elles achetent chat en poche." [15] Whereas women are always able to satisfy men's needs, it may be otherwise when it is up to the men to satisfy theirs.

It is precisely this linking of passion and women that can help us comprehend many of Montaigne's antifeminist remarks. If the woman represents sex, she becomes a threat to Montaigne's self-possession; he says of sexual activity that it puts

> ...toute autre pensée soubs le joug, abrutit et abestit par son imperieuse authorité toute la theologie et philosophie

---

[12] *Ibid.,* p. 311.
[13] *Ibid.,* pp. 314-315.
[14] *Ibid.,* p. 315.
[15] *Ibid.,* p. 315.

> qui est en Platon.... Partout ailleurs vous pouvez garder quelque decence... cette-cy ne se peut pas seulement imaginer que vitieuse ou ridicule. [16]

The sexual paradox is a crucial one, for although he asks, "qu'a faict l'action genitale aux hommes, si naturelle, si necessaire et si juste, pour n'en oser parler sans vergongne et pour l'exclurre des propos serieux et reglez?," [17] he also claims that sexuality absorbs and dissipates the faculties of our minds: "Certes, c'est une marque non seulement de nostre corruption originelle, mais aussi de nostre vanité et deformité." [18] In this respect, sexuality and love (which may be considered synonymous in the *Essais*) are seen as threats to male rationality. Montaigne admits that "Cupidon est un Dieu felon; il faict son jeu à luitter la devotion et la justice; c'est sa gloire, que sa puissance choque tout'autre puissance, et que tout autres regles cedent aux siennes." [19] And for one who has consistently advocated the cultivation of a self which does not yield and lose itself to others, love is seen as nothing less than a loss of self.

Montaigne struggles against "ces violentes passions," [20] "l'accointance des femmes, où l'incitation est violente et, dit-on par-fois invincible." [21] His own sex life is characterized by moderation rather than transport:

> ... en ce marché, je ne me laissois pas tout aller; je m'y plaisois, mais je ne m'y oubliois pas; je reservois en son entier ce peu de sens et de discretion que nature m'a donné, pour leur service et pour le mien; un peu d'esmotion, mais point de resverie. [22]

However, moderation does not solve the problem completely: "Les passions me sont autant aisées à eviter comme elles me sont difficiles à moderer." [23] The threat of desire's hold remains, for Montaigne already told us that his own nature is a passionate one which

---

[16] *Ibid.*, p. 306.
[17] *Ibid.*, p. 270.
[18] *Ibid.*, p. 306.
[19] *Ibid.*, p. 298.
[20] *Ibid.*, T. I, L. I, p. 11.
[21] *Ibid.*, T. II, L. III, p. 230.
[22] *Ibid.*, p. 321.
[23] *Ibid.*, p. 466.

he must control: "Je sens à temps les petits vents qui me viennent taster et bruire au dedans." [24] We may gain insight into this problem and Montaigne's possible resolutions by glancing at Maud Bodkin's psychological study of the image of woman in literature. Though she speaks of Milton, her conclusion appears quite applicable to Montaigne:

> ...the passionate nature of woman — or rather his own sense both of oneness with the passion he recognizes in woman and of superiority to it — makes her image the very projection of the weaker, more vulnerable part within himself. So she becomes a...symbol of the destructive power of passion conjoined with the will to rule. [25]

Within this context, let us glance at a few of Montaigne's discussions which prove unfavorable to women. He is aware that women's chastity (so necessary to masculine pride) is not simply a physical issue; it transcends the body to the will: "Est-ce la volonté que nous voulons qu'elles brident? C'est une piece bien souple et active; elle a beaucoup de promptitude pour la pouvoir arrester." [26] Since it seems so difficult to control women, one possible answer is to render them less desirable and powerful by attributing to them negative characteristics: "Leur essence est si confite en soubçon, en vanité et en curiosité, que de les guarir par voye legitime, il ne faut pas l'esperer." [27] He also claims that "la plus part de leurs deuils sont artificiels et ceremonieux." [28] Whereas we learned in Chapter III that he desired a woman only if she was a challenge, he says that women's chastity is easily corrupted by flattery. [29] What could be less complimentary and temptation-producing than the following declaration:

> D'autant que l'âme est plus vuide et sans contrepoids, elle se baisse plus facilement soubs la charge de la premiere persuasion. Voylà pourquoy les enfans, le vulgaire, les

---

[24] *Ibid.*, p. 463.
[25] Bodkin, pp. 169-170.
[26] Montaigne, T. II, L. III, pp. 291-292.
[27] *Ibid.*, p. 297.
[28] *Ibid.*, p. 250.
[29] *Ibid.*, T. II, L. II, p. 16.

> femmes et les malades sont plus subjects à estre menez par les oreilles. [30]

One way of resisting their attraction (though it may ironically serve to increase it) is to establish its impropriety: "... selon la loy que nature leur donne, ce n'est pas proprement à elles de vouloir et desirer; leur rolle est souffrir, obeir, consentir." [31] But in another section, he depicts their insatiable lust:

> Celles mesmes à qui la vieillesse refuse la force corporelle, fremissent encores, hannissent et tressaillent d'amour. Nous les voyons avant le faict pleines d'esperance et d'ardeur; et, quand le corps a joué son jeu, se chatouiller encor de la douceur de cette souvenance. [32]

Instead of finding that the male is at the mercy of the female's favors, he may convince himself that the reverse is true: "Elles ont toujours leur heure, afin qu'elles soyent tousjours prestes à la nostre: 'pati natæ' (nées pour subir-Sénèque)." [33] He makes it quite clear that women are objects created to be enjoyed by men:

> Ces encheriments deshontez que la chaleur premiere nous suggere en ce jeu, sont, non indecemment seulement, mais dommageablement employez envers noz femmes.... Elles sont toujours assez esveillées pour nostre *besoing*. [34] (Italics mine.)

This effect is heightened when he explains, "apprenons aux dames à se faire valoir, à s'estimer, à nous amuser et à nous piper." [35] When he does speak well of a woman, it is often as a result of her sacrifice for the male: he praises the "gentillesse" and "courage" of "gentilsfemmes qui ... d'un cœur magnanime s'aviserent de charger sur leurs espaules leurs maris, leurs enfans et le Duc mesme." [36] It is worthy of note that after this praise, he adds, and on the very

---

[30] *Ibid.*, T. I, L. I, p. 193.
[31] *Ibid.*, T. II, L. III, p. 314.
[32] *Ibid.*, p. 246.
[33] *Ibid.*, p. 314.
[34] *Ibid.*, T. I, L. I, pp. 226-227.
[35] *Ibid.*, T. II, L. III, p. 309.
[36] *Ibid.*, T. I, L. I, p. 4.

same page, "les natures plus foibles, comme celles des femmes, des enfans et du vulgaire..."[37]

Finally, Montaigne prefigures Freud's anatomical bias with the argument that a woman's physical structure provides the natural basis for her passivity:

> Et où elle [la nature] a voulu que nos appetis eussent montre et declaration prominante, ell'a faict que les leurs fussent occultes et intestins et les a fournies de pieces impropres à l'ostentation et simplement pour la defensive.[38]

In establishing that the woman must be a passive, receptive object, Montaigne assumes a temporary control over her ability to possess him. However, his attacks on women lead him into his own trap: "Il est bien plus aisé d'accuser l'un sexe, que d'excuser l'autre,"[39] especially when he returns to the theme of female sexuality:

> A quoy sert l'art de cette honte virginalle? cette froideur rassise, cette contenance severe, cette profession d'ignorance des choses qu'elles sçavent mieux que nous qui les en instruisons, qu'à nous accroistre le desir de vaincre, gourmander et fouler à nostre appetit toute cette ceremonie et ces obstacles? Car il y a non seulement du plaisir, mais de la gloire encore, d'affolir et desbaucher cette molle douceur et cette pudeur enfantine; et de ranger à la mercy de nostre ardeur une gravité fiere et magistrale.[40]

Paul Stapfer views Montaigne exclusively in the light of his denigrating remarks about women. He concludes that

> il n'y a vraiment aucune raison pour que les femmes se plaisent à la lecture de Montaigne: car il n'a guère dit sur leur compte que des impertinences, beaucoup d'incongruités et quelque sottises. Il a mal parlé de l'amour, qu'il n'a jamais envisagé par le grand côté de la passion, mais toujours par le petit côté du plaisir et de la bagatelle.[41]

---

[37] *Ibid.*, p. 4.

[38] *Ibid.*, T. II, L. III, p. 314. ("The dualism of masculine-feminine is merely the transposition into genital terms of the dualism of activity and passivity," Norman O. Brown, *Life Against Death*, p. 133.)

[39] *Ibid.*, p. 329.

[40] *Ibid.*, T. II, L. II, p. 12.

[41] Stapfer, p. 50.

But we must add that if Montaigne speaks ill of love, it is because he is guarding against its possible effects. Fortunat Strowski agrees that "ce fut la passion de l'amour qui fut le tourment de ces années d'apprentissage. Il a connu 'les étroits baisers de la jeunesse, savoureux, gloutons et gluants.' " [42] When Montaigne declares of women, "nostre maistrise et entiere possession leur est infiniement à craindre depuis qu'elles sont du tout rendues à la mercy de nostre foy et constance, elles sont un peu bien hasardées," [43] the fear of possession that he attempts to relegate to women is a fear that he knows at first hand. He tells us,

> c'est... pour moy un doux commerce que celuy des belles et honnestes femmes... mais c'est un commerce où il se faut tenir un peu sur ses gardes, et notamment ceux en qui le corps peut beaucoup, comme en moy. Je m'y eschauday en mon enfance et y souffris toutes les rages que les poëtes disent advenir à ceux qui s'y laissent aller sans ordre et sans jugement, [44]

and Strowski asserts that "il a connu l'impuissance provoquée par l'excès d'un désir trop véhément." [45] In an effort to overcome the fact that he is subject to the people and events around him ("et la plus penible assiete pour moy, c'est estre suspens ès choses qui pressent, et agité entre la crainte et l'esperance"), [46] Montaigne declares, "desprenons nous de toutes les liaisons qui nous attachent à autruy, gaignons sur nous de pouvoir à bon escient vivre seuls et y vivre à nostr'aise." [47]

Armaingaud exhibits a profound comprehension of Montaigne's need to control his desires:

> ...Montaigne a, tout le long de sa vie, lutté en général contre ses inclinations; ... opposé une résistance persévérante à l'amour passion. ...*De ménager sa volonté*, n'est-il pas d'ailleurs consacré tout entier à nous montrer comment

---

[42] Fortunat Strowski, *Montaigne, sa vie publique et privée* (Paris, 1938), p. 41.
[43] Montaigne, T. II, L. III, p. 310.
[44] *Ibid.*, pp. 244-245.
[45] Strowski, p. 42.
[46] Montaigne, T. II, L. II, p. 46.
[47] *Ibid.*, T. I, L. I, p. 270.

il a ... employé avec succès tous ses efforts à rester maître de ses impulsions, de ses passions, et à ne jamais s'en laisser posséder? [48]

Montaigne himself lets us know that he is extremely vulnerable: "J'ay esté tousjours chatouilleux et delicat aux offences; je suis plus tendre à cette heure, et ouvert par tout..." [49] And when it comes to personal relationships, he is not quite happy with himself: "...j'ay d'ailleurs quelques airs de la sotte honte dequoy parle Plutarque, et en a esté la cours de ma vie blessé et taché diversement. ...J'ay les yeux tendres à soustenir un refus, comme à refuser." [50] Once a man is aware of the coexistence within him of passions and vulnerability, he has a choice: to give himself to his emotions or to try to control them and become master of himself. There is little question as to which path Montaigne chose. He was by no means blind to the conflicts within him; he tells us, "on ne peut se vanter de mespriser et combattre la volupté, si on ne la voit, si on l'ignore, et ses graces, et ses forces, et sa beauté, plus attrayante. Je cognoy l'une et l'autre, c'est à moy à le dire." [51] Francis Jeanson explains that "il éprouve en lui-même un constant remue-ménage de sentiments et d'émotions; fasciné par ce monde intérieur, il pense avoir 'assez affaire à disposer et ranger' cette 'presse domestique' sans y adjoindre une 'presse estrangere.'" [52] His reading of the *Essais* leads him to state, "il est profondément attaché à soi, amoureux de lui-même." [53] But we must realize that the source of his preoccupation is a defensive one, stemming from the fact that "ne pouvant reigler les evenements, je me reigle moy-mesme," [54] from his fear of other people: "Par tout cela j'ay prins à haine mortelle d'estre tenu ny à autre, ny par autre que moy." [55] In his awareness of flux and inconstancy ("le pis que je trouve en nostre estat, c'est l'instabilité..."), [56] Montaigne sought a fixed point of

---

[48] Montaigne, *Oeuvres Complètes*, I, p. 99.
[49] Montaigne, T. II, L. III, p. 265.
[50] *Ibid.*, p. 292.
[51] *Ibid.*, p. 236.
[52] Francis Jeanson, *Montaigne par lui-même* (Paris 1964), p. 72.
[53] *Ibid.*, p. 72.
[54] Montaigne, T. II, L. II, p. 46.
[55] *Ibid.*, T. II, L. III, p. 409.
[56] *Ibid.*, T. II, L. II, p. 59.

stability which could provide for him security and freedom from turmoil: this point was the self.

The first page of the *Essais* makes it clear that he wishes to transform the potentially chaotic currents of his existence into the solidity of a book: "... c'est moy que je peins ... je suis moy-mesme la matiere de mon livre." [57] In effect, one of the functions of the *Essais* is that in writing, Montaigne molds his "moi":

> Me peignant pour autruy, je me suis peint en moy de couleurs plus nettes que n'estoyent les miennes premieres. Je n'ay pas plus faict mon livre que mon livre m'a faict, livre consubstantiel à son autheur, d'une occupation propre, membre de ma vie. [58]

It is because he is aware that "le monde n'est qu'une branloire perenne. ... Je ne puis asseurer mon object" [59] that he admits, "si mon ame pouvoit prendre pied, je ne m'essaierois pas, je me resoudrois." [60] The *Essais* can be viewed as Montaigne's attempt (essai) to resolve himself, to establish a personality as solid as a book. We may find a confirmation of this possibility when he exclaims, "j'ay faict ce que j'ay voulu: tout le monde me reconnoit en mon livre, et mon livre en moy." [61] But his aspiration towards solidity is threatened by passion:

> On ne peut desavouër et desdire les vices qui nous surprennent et vers lesquels les passions nous emportent; mais ceux qui par longue habitude sont *enracinés* et *ancrés*, en une volonté forte et vigoureuse, ne sont subjects à contradiction. [62] (Italics mine.)

Maurice Merleau-Ponty in his "Lecture de Montaigne" offers a brilliant analysis of Montaigne's obsession with the self: "La conscience de soi est sa constante, la mesure pour lui de toutes les doctrines. On pourrait dire qu'il n'est jamais sorti d'un certain étonnement devant soi qui fait toute la substance de son œuvre et de sa

---

[57] *Ibid.*, T. I, p. 1.
[58] *Ibid.*, T. II, L. II, p. 69.
[59] *Ibid.*, T. II, L. III, p. 222.
[60] *Ibid.*, p. 222.
[61] *Ibid.*, p. 303.
[62] *Ibid.*, p. 226.

sagesse." [63] But we must ask whether this obsession is the result of a strong sense of self or a basic lack of one? Montaigne tells us,

> je ne me tiens pas bien en ma possession et disposition. Le hazard y a plus de droict que moy. L'occasion, la compaignie, le branle mesme de ma voix tire plus de mon esprit que je n'y trouve lors que je le sonde et employe à part moy, [64]

and Merleau-Ponty proves to be the most perceptive critic in realizing that "il ne connaît pas ce lieu de repos, cette possession de soi..." [65] If we accept this remark as a possible foundation for Montaigne's cult of the self, we understand that his primary goal is to achieve the "repos" which can only be obtained through self-sufficiency: "Je me contente de jouïr le monde sans m'en empresser, de vivre une vie seulement excusable, et qui seulement ne poise ny à moy, ny à autruy." [66] To reach this end, he must liberate himself from the hold of people outside him: "Il faut desnoüer ces obligations si fortes, et... n'espouser rien que soy." [67] This is where the conflict with woman is put in relief, for he has made it obvious that she and her passion constitute the greatest threat to his liberty and self-development. As he confesses, "mais aux affections qui me distrayent de moy et attachent ailleurs, à celles là certes m'oppose-je de toute ma force." [68]

"Autruy" (especially the opposite sex) is equivalent to instability for Montaigne: "De fonder la recompense des actions vertueuses sur l'approbation d'autruy, c'est prendre un trop incertain et trouble fondement." [69] We find him "fuyant mortellement la servitude et l'obligation" [70] and also fleeing intimacy with others, substituting for it the magnetic attraction of self-analysis:

---

[63] Maurice Merleau-Ponty, "Lecture de Montaigne," *Les Temps Modernes* (December, 1947), p. 1045.
[64] Montaigne, T. I, L. I, p. 37.
[65] Merleau-Ponty, p. 1045.
[66] Montaigne, T. II, L. III, p. 389.
[67] *Ibid.*, T. I, L. I, p. 272.
[68] *Ibid.*, T. II, L. III, p. 447.
[69] *Ibid.*, p. 225.
[70] *Ibid.*, p. 243.

> Chacun regarde devant soy; moy, je regarde dedans moy:
> je n'ay affaire qu'à moy, je me considere sans cesse, je me
> contrerolle, je me gouste... je me roulle en moy mesme. [71]

In limiting his responsibility to his own existence, he fulfills his concept of liberty in detachment: "Je... ne vis que pour moy: mes desseins se terminent là." [72] Above all, Montaigne does not want to suffer or be suffered for; his goal, as I have mentioned, is self-sufficiency. He complains, "vous souffrez pour autruy, ou autruy pour vous; l'un et l'autre inconvenient est poisant, mais le dernier me semble encore plus rude." [73]

Jeanson sees in this self-development a glaring selfishness:

> Sa tolérance, son respect des opinions d'autrui, c'est une
> indifférence à peu près totale à l'égard de ces opinions,
> dans la mesure du moins où elles ne le concernent pas lui-
> même. Cet 'humaniste' n'aime pas les hommes: il s'aime
> à travers eux, il a besoin d'eux pour se rencontrer. ...Il
> vit bien; il ne manque de rien; il peut se consacrer à soi. [74]

His analysis is substantiated by the fact that Montaigne seems incapable of sacrificing for others, much as he approves of this capacity in women. In speaking of his father, he tells us, "il ne fut jamais ame plus charitable et populaire. Ce train, que je louë en autruy, je n'aime point à le suivre, et ne suis pas sans excuse." [75] He even declares, "j'ay grand soin d'augmenter par estude et par discours ce privilege d'insensibilité, qui est naturellement bien avancé en moy." [76]

The *Essais* leave no question that Montaigne's search for self-possession is equivalent to a search for "repos" ("l'esprit se tenant tousjours en repos et en santé... sans vexation, sans passion"). [77] For him, the self is not a phenomenon that responds openly to the world around it, but a refuge, secure in its isolation: "Deliberé autant que je pourroy, ne me mesler d'autre chose que de passer

---

[71] *Ibid.*, T. II, L. II, p. 61.
[72] *Ibid.*, T. II, L. III, p. 250.
[73] *Ibid.*, p. 429.
[74] Jeanson, p. 81.
[75] Montaigne, T. II, L. III, p. 450.
[76] *Ibid.*, p. 447.
[77] *Ibid.*, p. 452.

en repos et à part ce peu qui me reste de vie, ... s'entretenir soy mesmes, et s'arrester et rasseoir en soy." [78] There is little room for women in the life of a man who channels everything "au repos de mon esprit et à moy." [79] Ultimately, it is his fear of the turmoil of living, of the "inquietude" and "irresolution" that are "nos maistresses qualitez, et prædominantes" [80] that lead him to reject the world of women and passion. In this respect, he calls to mind Madame de la Fayette's *La Princesse de Clèves*; one century later, the problem of the Princess resembles that of Montaigne. Caught between the turmoil and insecurity of love and the desire for her "repos," she sacrifices her passion to her need for untroubled tranquillity.

Montaigne's overriding wish is also for "repos" and he confesses, "j'ayme à ne sçavoir pas le conte de ce que j'ay, pour sentir moins exactement ma perte." [81] If he doesn't risk anything, he doesn't lose anything, and it is precisely the possibility of losing something (such as himself) that scares him most: "L'horreur de la cheute me donne plus de fiebvre que le coup." [82] He goes so far as to admit,

> la plus basse marche est la plus ferme. C'est le siege de la constance. Vous n'y avez besoing que de vous. Elle se fonde là et appuye toute en soy. [83]

This comment seems to represent Montaigne at his most honest and vulnerable: the constancy of self-sufficiency, though it may be the lowest rung on the ladder, constitutes the untroubled calm he requires. Whatever a woman may have represented for him, it was not security. It is quite possible that certain anti-feminist attitudes in the *Essais* may have stemmed from a need born of insecurity. Montaigne feared the potential power of a woman's intimacy; as Bodkin puts it, "the tyrannous grasp upon man's emotion possessed by the dynamic image of woman in its aspect as cherishing, sa-

---

[78] *Ibid.*, T. I, L. I, p. 29.
[79] *Ibid.* T. II, L. II, p. 61.
[80] *Ibid.*, T. II, L. III, p. 431.
[81] *Ibid.*, T. II, L. II, p. 45.
[82] *Ibid.*, p. 46.
[83] *Ibid.*, pp. 46-47.

tisfying, exalting, adds to the terror of its other aspect as enslaving, betraying." [84]

Therefore, rather than be enslaved or betrayed by a member of the opposite sex, he chose to control his passion and diminish the attraction she had for him. In order to achieve the "repos de sa conscience et d'autres passions intestines," [85] the state where his soul "est renduë maistresse de ses passions et concupiscences, maistresse de l'indigence, de la honte, de la pauvreté et de toutes autres injures de fortune," [86] he had to construct an impermeable "moi." He had to declare, "la plus grande chose du monde, c'est de sçavoir estre à soy" [87] in order to be safe from the uncertainty of relationships that demand and change. He had to have a wife whose essential function was to assume all practical responsibility, for he aspired to an existence where "nul desir, nulle crainte ou doubte qui luy trouble l'air, aucune difficulté passée, presente, future, par dessus laquelle son imagination ne passe sans offence." [88] Bonnefon agrees that

> il en arrivait insensiblement à ne considérer presque que le souci exclusif de son repos, trouvant un plaisir égoïste, un dilettantisme peu généreux à analyser ce repos, à sentir combien peu de choses pourraient le troubler. [89]

Given his interior Utopia, the "meilleure munition que j'aye trouvé à cet humain voyage" [90] is not love, or companionship, or good deeds, but books. And why books? Simply because they are safe, they are constant, they are a source of pleasure minus the risks of human interaction; unlike love, they are not "attizé par la difficulté." [91] Montaigne is altogether honest about his attachment to books:

---

[84] Bodkin, p. 173.
[85] Montaigne, T. II, L. III, p. 573.
[86] *Ibid.*, T. I, L. I, p. 93.
[87] *Ibid.*, p. 273.
[88] *Ibid.*, T. II, L. III, p. 573.
[89] Bonnefon, p. 293.
[90] Montaigne, T. II, L. III, p. 248.
[91] *Ibid.*, p. 278.

> J'en jouys, comme les avaritieux des tresors pour sçavoir que j'en jouyray quand il me plaira; mon ame se rassasie et contente de ce droict de possession. [92]

Books constitute a secure possession while women are inconstant, have needs of their own, and are, in some cases, not to be possessed (in the wider sense of the word). Montaigne is in control when he reads, as opposed to the fact that "cette aspreté et violence de desir empesche, plus qu'elle ne sert, à la conduitte de ce qu'en entreprend. ... Nous ne conduisons jamais bien la chose de laquelle nous sommes possedez et conduicts." [93] This phrase comes from the chapter entitled "De mesnager sa volonté," a title indicative of Montaigne's wish, especially when compared to the chapter title, "Nos affections s'emportent au delà de nous."

The way in which our passions take us out of ourselves, the literal ecstasy (from the Greek "exstasis" — displacement, movement out of one's self) evidently represents a threat to one whose sense of self is tenuous and uncertain, one who yearns for peaceful solidity. Montaigne constantly ascertains that this ecstasy is fundamentally sexual in nature. As Merleau-Ponty so intelligently puts it, "les passions paraissaient être la mort du moi, puisqu'elles l'emportent hors de lui-même, et Montaigne se sentait menacé par elles comme par la mort." [94] It is for this reason that Montaigne cannot let himself go; he is not sure what, if anything, he would return to. It is rather interesting that the only time he discusses letting go is in the context of dying. In fact, he equates "se laisser aller" with death as he regains consciousness after a bad fall:

> Il me sembloit que ma vie ne me tenoit plus qu'au bout des lévres; je fermois les yeux pour ayder, ce me sembloit, à la pousser hors, et prenois plaisir à m'alanguir et à me laisser aller. ... Je croy que c'est ce mesme estat où se trouvent ceux qu'on voit défaillans de foiblesse en l'agonie de la mort. [95]

---

[92] *Ibid.*, p. 248.
[93] *Ibid.*, p. 452.
[94] Merleau-Ponty, p. 1058.
[95] Montaigne, T. I, L. II, pp. 409-410.

"Se laisser aller" is the liberation of the body from the rigorous (though not altogether successful) hold of the mind: "Si le corps se gouvernoit autant selon moy que faict l'ame, nous marcherions un peu plus à nostre aise." [96] In this respect, the *Essais* can be interpreted as an attempt on Montaigne's part to overcome the physical element with the philosophical, or to at least incorporate the body in such a way that it is no longer threatening. It appears that he even controlled his appetite for food to the point that "l'appetit me vient en mangeant, et point autrement; je n'ay point de faim qu'à table." [97] Merleau-Ponty explains that "le remède à la mort et aux passions n'est pas de s'en détourner, mais au contraire de passer au delà comme tout nous y porte. ... Toute sa morale repose sur un mouvement de fierté par lequel il décide de prendre en mains sa vie hasardeuse ..." [98] Montaigne's work can be seen as the triumph of the male virtue of rationality (the head) over the female threat of passion (the body).

Since man is an embodied creature, the self is therefore an embodied entity. Consequently, the loss of self through enslavement to another is feared by Montaigne only when the sexual element exists. As Merleau-Ponty interprets the *Essais*, "c'est que notre corps et ses paisibles fonctions sont traversés par le pouvoir que nous avons de nous vouer à autre chose et de nous donner des absolus." [99] For as we saw with Mademoiselle de Gournay and as we shall now see with La Boétie, Montaigne was not incapable of attachment as long as there was no physical threat. When Montaigne speaks of his relationship with La Boétie, he depicts a union so complete that there was, in fact, a loss of self: "En l'amitié dequoy je parle, elles [nos âmes] se meslent et confondent l'une en l'autre, d'un melange si universel, qu'elles effacent et ne retrouvent plus la couture qui les a jointes." [100] But although there was a loss, it was a mutual one in which there was no risk of being "possessed" by the other:

---

[96] *Ibid.*, T. II, L. III, p. 555.
[97] *Ibid.*, T. II, L. III, p. 415.
[98] Merleau-Ponty, p. 1059.
[99] *Ibid.*, p. 1047.
[100] Montaigne, T. I, L. I, pp. 203-204.

> C'est je ne sçay quelle quinte essence de tout ce meslange, qui, ayant saisi toute ma volonté, l'amena se plonger et se perdre dans la sienne; qui, ayant saisi toute sa volonté, l'amena se plonger et se perdre en la mienne, d'une faim, d'une concurrence pareille. Je dis perdre, à la verité, ne nous reservant rien qui nous fut propre, ny qui fut ou sien, ou mien. [101]

Montaigne lost his individuality but, as far as we know, sexual passion played no part. If Montaigne's loss of self was so great without the physical element, can there be any doubt as to the intensity that would result from the addition of sexuality? For Montaigne, involving the body as well as the soul would have made the union too complete for comfort. Perhaps it is for this reason that he insists that one woman cannot be both mistress and wife to a man; he declares, "... il y a danger que l'amitié qu'on porte à une telle femme soit immoderée: car si l'affection maritalle s'y trouve entiere et perfaite, comme elle doit, et qu'on la surcharge encore de celle qu'on doit à la parantelle, il n'y a point de doubte que ce surcroist n'emporte un tel mary hors les barrieres de la raison." [102] There is once again a threat in the double power of mistress and friend merged in one woman. Frame sees in the *Essais* that "love is dangerous. ... Our pleasure should be restrained, serious, and austere; since the aim of marriage is generation, perhaps we should not make love to our wives except for that purpose." [103] He adds that despite Montaigne's frankness, he was bashful about showing his body. Frame refers us to Florimond de Raemond, Montaigne's friend and successor in Parliament, who wrote on his copy of the *Essais*:

> I have often heard the author (Montaigne) say that although he, full of love, ardor, and youth, had married his very beautiful and very lovable wife, yet the fact is that he had never played with her except with respect for the honor that the marriage bed requires, without ever having seen anything but her hands and face uncovered, and not even her breast, although among other women he was extremely playful and debauched. [104]

---

[101] *Ibid.*, p. 204.
[102] *Ibid.*, p. 226.
[103] Frame, p. 92.
[104] *Ibid.*, p. 93.

It seems that Montaigne exercised extreme restraint to keep from the intensity of sexual pleasure.

Ruth Kelso suggests that marital reserve was common during the Renaissance since men tried to decrease female sexuality, based on their fear of being cuckolded:

> The great danger, men were warned, was that the girl who came to the marriage bed a virgin in body and mind might become debauched by the excesses and lack of modesty of her own husband. A husband who inflames his wife is to blame if afterwards she admits a lover. ... He must treat her as a husband and not as a lover. ... Many writers would have eliminated all pleasure from the marital act if they could, and went so far even as to recommend methods that insure the least possible satisfaction to the wife. [105]

However, we noted earlier that cuckoldry was not one of Montaigne's fears. The threat was not a phallic one; it was rather the problem of identity and the self, with its source less in that which makes him a man than in that which renders him a human being. It is a threat which can be shared by women since it poses questions such as: how does one give of oneself to others without losing one's selfhood? How does one remain open to the needs of loved ones without necessarily living for them? Can one be simultaneously free and involved, independent and passionate? The answer offered by Montaigne's life is that he never managed to achieve selfhood without robbing women of their power. We should not forget that his negative reactions to the passionate experiences of his youth were perfectly in keeping with the Renaissance sensibility and its emphasis on "sagesse" over physicality. The phenomenon of the new "rational animal" is well described by Simone de Beauvoir in *The Ethics of Ambiguity*: "He escapes from his natural condition without, however, freeing himself from it. ... He asserts himself as a pure internality against which no external power can take hold ..." [106] And in the light of Montaigne's aforementioned need for solidity and certainty,

---

[105] Ruth Kelso, *Doctrine for the Lady of the Renaissance* (Urbana, 1956), pp. 87-88.

[106] Simone de Beauvoir, *The Ethics of Ambiguity*, trans. Bernard Frechtman (New York, 1948), p. 7.

> la sagesse est un bastiment solide et entier, dont chaque piece tient son rang et porte sa marque. ... Je laisse aux artistes ... [d'] arrester nostre inconstance et la mettre par ordre. [107]

The self-sufficiency and "repos" to which Montaigne aspired could be obtained only at the price of subjugating his body and its desires, and of limiting women's field of possibility till it was no longer threatening. It was from a lack of self ("... je crains mortellement d'estre pris en eschange par ceux à qui il arrive de connoistre mon nom" [108]) rather than a plenitude that he limited his own experience to that which was secure and free from care. By the same token, it was not the inherent inferiority of women, but his own fear of them, that led Montaigne towards the current of antifeminism.

---

[107] Montaigne, T. II, L. III, p. 530.
[108] *Ibid.*, p. 269.

CONCLUSION

After reading the *Essais*, we are left with as little right to define Montaigne as feminist or antifeminist as when we began: among all the contradictions that we and he find within him, many revolve around women. We have been witnesses to his defense of women, from their sexual to educational rights, a defense which would have placed him in the feminist camp during the Renaissance. We also learned of his close friendship with Marie de Gournay, one of the most ardent feminists of the century.

On the other hand, we cannot deny his strong antifeminist sentiments which tend to undercut any remarks favorable to women. He reflected certain Renaissance conceptions, such as women's insatiable lust, and the incompatability of love and marriage inherited from the Middle Ages. In both his private life and his writings, he displayed a lack of understanding of and respect for the opposite sex and this absence of sensitivity would certainly earn him the term of "male chauvinist" in our own time. But I have attempted to expose the psychological roots of his antifeminism, namely a fear of passion and a predominant need for security, constancy and calm. The chaos of his passionate youth was rejected for the peace of his philosophical manhood: " 'Si votre affection en l'amour est trop puissante, dissipez-la,' disent-ils; et disent vray, car je l'ay souvant essayé avec utilité." [1] Antifeminism was a necessary means toward the dissipation of love and the control of both women and his own passionate nature. He offers us the fruit of his experience:

---

[1] Montaigne, T. II, L. III, p. 256.

CONCLUSION

> Si chacun espioit de près les effects et circonstances des passions qui le regentent, comme j'ay faict de celle à qui j'estoit tombé en partage, il les verroit venir, et ralantiroit un peu leur impetuosité et leur course.[2]

Having learned the folly of love and the virtue of moderation from antiquity, he made great efforts to restrain himself:

> Je me presche il y a si long temps de me tenir à moy, et separer des choses estrangeres; ... Or à un esprit si indocile, il faut des bastonnades; et faut rebattre et resserrer à bons coups de mail ce vaisseau qui se desprent, se descourt, qui s'eschape et desrobe de soy.[3]

Strowski offers us an image of Montaigne's youth which may serve as a clue to his need to "tenir mon ame et mes pensées en repos":[4]

> ... le jeune, l'ardent, le passionné, l'éblouissant Michel de Montaigne est un inquiet. *L'inquiétude* est son tourment et son ferment: inquiétude morale, inquiétude intellectuelle, inquiétude physique. L'inquiétude agite son corps, son imagination, sa volonté.[5]

To overcome the "inquiétude" and instability of his existence, Montaigne tried to establish, through the *Essais,* a self which would define him, enclose him, and detach him from both the need for and needs of "autruy." In an attempt at self-sufficiency, he was severe with the passions which open and give us to others, and with the woman who represented this aspect of life. But as Merleau-Ponty reminds us, "la critique des passions ne leur ôte pas la valeur, si elle va jusqu'à montrer que jamais nous ne sommes en possession de nous-mêmes et que la passion est nous."[6]

Despite Montaigne's partiality to paradox, towards the end of the *Essais* he seemed more inclined to make his peace with sensuality. Although he did not abandon his belief that "nous ne sentons

---

[2] *Ibid.,* p. 527.
[3] *Ibid.,* pp. 494-495.
[4] *Ibid.,* p. 467.
[5] Strowski, p. 47.
[6] Merleau-Ponty, p. 1055.

rien de plus doux en la vie qu'un repos et sommeil tranquille et profond, sans songes," [7] he was able to see passion through kinder eyes:

> Moy, ... hay cette inhumaine sapience qui nous veut rendre desdaigneux et ennemis de la culture du corps. J'estime pareille injustice prendre à contre coeur les voluptez naturelles que de les prendre trop à coeur. [8]

This is the view of an aging man who no longer requires the temperance of his earlier years. Whereas Montaigne used to associate sensuality with loss of self, he is now able to declare:

> Y a il quelque volupté qui me chatouille? je ne la laisse par friponer aux sens, j'y associe mon ame, ... non pas pour s'y perdre, mais pour s'y trouver. [9]

Although he still elevates the mind above the body at the end of his life,

> Socrates ... prise, comme il doit, la volupté corporelle, mais il prefere celle de l'esprit, comme ayant plus de force, de constance, de facilité, de varieté, de dignité, [10]

he is more appreciative of passion, probably because his body is no longer a threat to his self-possession. In fact, we find that the body now serves as a deterrent to the thought: "Que l'esprit esveille et vivifie la pesanteur du corps, le corps arreste la legereté de l'esprit et la fixe." [11] John Lapp perceives that "now his enfeebled body fears and provides adequate warning of excess, replacing the soul as counsellor of caution and discipline. The approach of old age thus reverses the former order." [12]

Finally, if we accept that Montaigne was interested in improving the quality of human life through self-analysis, and that the

---

[7] Montaigne, T. II, L. III, p. 503.
[8] *Ibid.*, p. 566.
[9] *Ibid.*, p. 573.
[10] *Ibid.*, p. 575.
[11] *Ibid.*, p. 575.
[12] John Lapp, "Montaigne's 'Négligence,'" *The Romanic Review*, LXI (October, 1970), p. 175.

seeds for equality between the sexes do exist in the *Essais,* we should read his precepts for good living as intended for all human beings. In this sense, he denounces female servitude (perhaps without even realizing it): to one whose existence is justified solely in terms of her husband's needs, he declares,

> comme qui oublieroit de bien et saintement vivre, et penseroit estre quite de son devoir en y acheminant et dressant les autres, ce seroit un sot; ... qui abandonne en son propre le sainement et gayement vivre pour en servir autruy, prent à mon gré un mauvais et desnaturé parti.[13]

Let us conclude with the following call to freedom,

> Dieu veuille que cet excès de ma licence attire nos hommes jusques à la liberté, par dessus ces vertus couardes et mineuses nées de nos imperfections; qu'aux despens de mon immoderation je les attire jusques au point de la raison![14]

and be aware that had Montaigne been less afraid of passion and its embodiment in women, and less preoccupied with himself and his "repos," he would have intended this statement not simply for men, but for the other half of humankind as well.

---

[13] Montaigne, T. II, L. III, p. 451.
[14] Ibid., pp. 267-268.

SELECTED BIBLIOGRAPHY

Abensour, Léon. *La Femme et le féminisme avant la Révolution.* Paris: Editions Ernest Leroux, 1923.
———. *Histoire générale du féminisme des origines à nos jours.* Paris: Delagrave, 1921.
Abercrombie, Nigel. *Saint Augustine and French Classical Thought.* Oxford: The Clarendon Press, 1938.
Armaingaud, Dr. Arthur. *Montaigne pamphlétaire. L'énigme du Contr'un.* Paris: Hachette et Cie., 1910.
Ascoli, Georges. "Essai sur l'histoire des idées féministes en France du XVIe siècle à la Révolution," *Revue de Synthèse Historique* (Juillet à Décembre, 1906).
Auerbach, Erich. "L'Humaine Condition," *Mimesis: The Representation of Reality in Western Literature.* Translated by Willard R. Trask. Princeton: Princeton University Press, 1953.
Bailey, Cyril. *Lucretius on the Nature of Things.* Oxford: Clarendon Press, 1921.
Baraz, Michaël. *L'Etre et la connaissance selon Montaigne.* Toulouse: Librairie José Corti, 1968.
———. "Les Images dans les *Essais* de Montaigne," *Bulletin d'Humanisme et Renaissance,* XXVII (1965).
Barrow, Reginald H. *Plutarch and His Times.* Bloomington: Indiana University Press, 1967.
Beauvoir, Simone de. *The Ethics of Ambiguity.* Translated by Bernard Frechtman. New York: Philosophical Library, 1948.
———. *The Second Sex.* Translated by H. M. Parshley. New York: Alfred A. Knopf, 1953.
Biot, Jean-Baptiste. *Mélanges scientifiques et littéraires.* Paris: Michel Lévy Frères, 1858.
Boase, Alan M. *The Fortunes of Montaigne: A History of the Essays in France.* London: Methuen & Co., Ltd., 1935.
Bodkin, Maud. *Archetypal Patterns in Poetry: Psychological Studies of Imagination.* London: Oxford University Press, 1965.
Bonnefon, Paul. *Montaigne, l'homme et l'œuvre.* Bordeaux: G. Gounouilhon, 1893.
———. *Montaigne et ses amis.* 2 vols. Genève: Slatkine Reprints, 1969.
Borel, Pierre, *Autour de Montaigne: Etudes littéraires.* Neuchâtel: Delachaux & Niestlé, 1945.
Bouchot, Henri F. *Les Femmes de Brantôme.* Paris: Maison Quantin, 1890.

Brantôme, Pierre de Bourdeilles. *Vies des dames illustres françoises et etrangères.* Paris: Librairie Garnier Frerès, 1920.
Brown, Norman O. *Life Against Death: The Psychoanalytical Meaning of History.* Middletown: Wesleyan University Press, 1959.
Brush, Craig B. *Montaigne and Bayle: Variations on the Theme of Skepticism.* The Hague: Martinus Nijhoff, 1966.
Buffum, Imbrie. *Studies in the Baroque from Montaigne to Rotrou.* New Haven: Yale University Press, 1957.
Burckhardt, Jacob. *The Civilization of the Renaissance in Italy.* Translated by S. G. C. Middlemore. London: Allen & Unwin, Ltd., 1960.
Butor, Michel. *Essais sur les 'Essais'.* Paris: Editions Gallimard, 1968.
Cabeen, David C. "Michel Eyquem de Montaigne," *A Critical Bibliography of French Literature.* Vol. II. Syracuse: Syracuse University Press, 1956.
Casevitz, Thérèse. "Mademoiselle de Gournay et le féminisme," *Revue Politique et Littéraire,* LXI (Décembre, 1925).
Castiglione, Baldassare. *The Book of the Courtier.* Translated by Sir Thomas Hoby. New York: AMS Press, 1967.
Catullus, C. Valerius. *Odi et Amo: The Complete Poetry of Catullus.* Translated by Roy Arthur Swanson. New York: The Liberal Arts Press, 1959.
Chartier, Alain. *La Belle dame sans mercy.* Paris: Librairie Droz, 1945.
Chastel, André and Klein, Robert. "L'Europe de la Renaissance," *L'Age de l'humanisme.* Bruxelles: Editions de la Connaissance, 1954.
Chateau, Jean. *Montaigne: psychologue et pédagogue.* Paris: Librairie Philosophique J. Vrin, 1964.
Chenot, Anna Adele. "Marie de Gournay, Feminist and Friend of Montaigne," *Poet Lore,* XXXIV (January-December, 1923).
Cioranescu, Alexandre. *Bibliographie de la littérature française du seizième siècle.* Paris: C. Klincksieck, 1959.
Conche, Marcel. *Montaigne ou la conscience heureuse.* Paris: Editions Seghers, 1964.
Corraze, Raymond. "Les Lopez, ancêtres maternels de Michel de Montaigne," *Travaux historiques et scientifiques. Bulletin philologique et historique* (1932/33).
Courteault, Paul. "La Mère de Montaigne," *Revue historique de Bordeaux et du département de la Gironde,* XXVII (Janvier-Février, 1934 and Mars-Avril, 1934).
Crenne, Hélisenne de. *Les Angoysses douloureuses qui procèdent d'amours.* Edited by Paule Demats. Paris: Les Belles Lettres, 1968.
Crocker, Lester G. *The Selected Essays of Montaigne.* New York: Pocket Library, 1959.
Crump, Marjorie M. *The Growth of the Aeneid.* Oxford: Basil Blackwell, 1920.
Dédéyan, Charles. *Essais sur le Journal de voyage de Montaigne.* Paris: Boivin & Cie., [194-].
Doumic, René. "L'Egoïsme de Montaigne," *Etudes sur la littérature française.* Sér. I. Paris: Perrin et Cie., 1896.
Dowden, Edward. *Michel de Montaigne.* Philadelphia: J. B. Lippincott Co., 1905.
Dresden, Samuel. *Humanism in the Renaissance.* New York: McGraw-Hill Co., 1968.
Drew, D. L. *The Allegory of the Aeneid.* Oxford: Basil Blackwell, 1927.
Dupin, Henri. *La Courtoisie au Moyen Age.* Paris: Picard, 1906.

Erasmus, Desiderius. *The Colloquies of Erasmus.* Translated by Craig G. Thompson. Chicago: University of Chicago Press, 1965.
Faguet, Emile. *Seizième siècle: Etudes littéraires.* Paris: Boivin & Cie., 1936.
Faral, Edmond. "Le Roman de la Rose et la pensée française au XIIIe siècle," *Revue des Deux Mondes* (Séptembre, 1926).
Faure, Elie. *Montaigne et ses trois premiers-nés.* Paris: G. Crès et Cie., 1926.
Festugière, Jean. *La Philosophie de l'amour de Marsille Ficin et son influence sur la littérature française au XVIe siècle.* Paris: Librairie Philosophique J. Vrin, 1941.
Feugère, Léon Jacques. *Etienne de La Boëtie, ami de Montaigne.* Paris: J. Labitte, 1845.
———. *Les Femmes poëtes au XVIe siècle.* Paris: Didier et Cie., 1860.
Frame, Donald M. *Montaigne: A Biography.* New York: Harcourt, Brace & World, Inc., 1965.
———. *Montaigne's Discovery of Man: The Humanization of a Humanist.* New York: Columbia University Press, 1955.
———. *Montaigne in France.* New York: Columbia University Press, 1940.
Frappier, Jean. *La Poésie lyrique en France au XIIe et XIIIe siècles.* Paris: Centre de documentation universitaire, 1962.
Freud, Sigmund. *The Ego and the Id.* Translated by Joan Riviere. New York: W. W. Norton & Co., Inc., 1962.
———. *An Outline of Psychoanalysis.* Translated by James Strachey. New York: W. W. Norton & Co., Inc., 1949.
Friedrich, Hugo. *Montaigne.* Translated by Robert Rovini. Paris: Gallimard, 1968.
Gide, André. *Essais sur Montaigne.* Paris: J. Schriffin, 1929.
Giraud, Victor. *Maîtres d'autrefois et d'aujourd'hui.* Paris: Hachette, 1914.
Gournay, Marie de. *Egalité des hommes et des femmes.* In Schiff, Mario, *La Fille d'alliance de Montaigne, Marie de Gournay.* Paris: Honoré Champion, 1910.
———. *Grief des dames.* In Schiff, Mario, *La Fille d'alliance de Montaigne, Marie de Gournay.* Paris: Honoré Champion, 1910.
———. *Les Idées littéraires de Mlle de Gournay.* Edited by Anne Uildriks. Groningen: n.p., 1926.
———. *Le Provmenoir de Monsievr de Montaigne. Par sa fille d'alliance.* Paris: Abel L'Angelier, 1594.
Guérin, Eugénie de. *Lettres à son frère Maurice.* Paris: J. Gabalda et Fils, 1929.
Guizot, Guillaume. *Montaigne: Etudes et fragments.* Paris: Librairie Hachette, 1899.
Hallie, Philip Paul. *The Scar of Montaigne.* Middletown: Wesleyan University Press, 1966.
Hannay, David. *The Later Renaissance.* London: William Blackwood and Sons, 1911.
Hay, Camilla Hill. *Montaigne lecteur et imitateur de Sénèque.* Poitiers: Société française de l'imprimerie et de librairie, 1938.
Hermant Paul. "Le Sentiment amoureux dans la littérature médiévale," *Revue de Synthèse Historique,* XII (Janvier-Juin, 1906).
Hodgson, Geraldine. *Studies in French Education from Rabelais to Rousseau.* New York: Burt Franklin, 1969.
Hudleston, F. J. "Montaigne's Adopted Daughter," *Living Age,* VI (July, 1895).

Ilsley, Marjorie. *A Daughter of the Renaissance, Marie le Jars de Gournay: Her Life and Her Works.* The Hague: Mouton & Co., 1963.
Jansen, Frederik Julius. *Sources vives de la pensée de Montaigne.* Copenhagen: Levin & Munksgaard, 1935.
Jeanson, Francis. *Montaigne par lui-même.* Paris: Editions du Seuil, 1964.
Joran, Théodore. *Les Féministes avant le féminisme.* Paris: Gabriel Beauchesne, 1935.
Kelso, Ruth. *Doctrine for the Lady of the Renaissance.* Urbana: University of Illinois Press, 1956.
La Charité, Raymond C. *The Concept of Judgment in Montaigne.* The Hague: Martinus Nijhoff, 1968.
Lamandé, André. "La Jeunesse de Montaigne," *Revue de France,* VI (1927).
———. *La Vie gaillarde et sage de Montaigne.* Paris: Les Petits-fils de Plon et Nourrit, 1927.
Langlois, Ernest. *Origines et Sources du Roman de la Rose.* Paris: Ernest Thorin, 1891.
Lanson, Gustave. *Les Essais de Montaigne: Etude et analyse.* Paris: Mellottée, 1930.
Lapp, John. "Montaigne's 'Négligence,'" *The Romanic Review,* LXI (October, 1970).
Laumonier, Paul. "Madame de Montaigne d'après les *'Essais',*" *Mélanges offerts à M. Abel Lefranc.* Paris: E. Droz, 1936.
Lazar, Moshé. *Amour Courtois et "Fin'Amors" dans la littérature du XIIe siècle.* Paris: Librairie C. Klincksieck, 1964.
Lefranc, Abel. *Grands écrivains français de la Renaissance.* Paris: Eduard Champion, 1914.
———. *Rabelais: Etudes sur Gargantua, Pantagruel, le Tiers Livre.* Paris: Editions Albin Michel, 1953.
———. *La Vie quotidienne au temps de la Renaissance.* Paris: Hachette, 1938.
Legouvé, Ernest. *The Moral History of Women.* New York: Rudd & Carleton, 1860.
Lenient, Charles Félix. *La Satire en France; ou la littérature militante au XVIe siècle.* Vol. I. Paris: Burt Franklin, 1877.
Leveaux, Alphonse. *Etude sur les Essais de Montaigne.* Paris: H. Plon, 1970.
Lewis, C. S. *The Allegory of Love: A Study in Medieval Tradition.* London: Oxford University Press, 1936.
Lorris, Guillaume de, et Meung, Jean de. *Le Roman de la Rose.* Paris: Félix Lecoy, 1968.
Loviot, Louis. "Hélisenne de Crenne," *Revue des livres anciens.* Paris: Fontemoing et Cie., 1917.
Lowndes, Mary Elizabeth. *Michel de Montaigne: A Bibliographical Study.* Cambridge: The University Press, 1968.
Luck, Georg. *The Latin Love Elegy.* New York: Methuen & Co., 1960.
Lucretius, Carus. *De Rerum Natura.* Translated by W. H. D. Rouse. Cambridge: Harvard University Press, 1937.
Malvezin, Théophile. *Michel de Montaigne, son origine, sa famille.* Bordeaux: C. Lefebvre, 1875.
Marcu, Eva. *Répertoire des idées de Montaigne.* Genève: Librairie Droz, 1965.
Marguerite de Navarre. *L'Heptaméron.* Paris: Garnier, 1964.

Marolles, Michel de. *Mémoires de Michel de Marolles, abbé de Villeoin.* Amsterdam: n.p., 1755.
Maulde la Clavière, Marie René de. *The Woman of the Renaissance: A Study of Feminism.* Translated by George Herbert Ely. New York: G. P. Putnam's Sons, 1905.
Mauzey, Jesse Virgil. *Montaigne's Philosophy of Human Nature.* Annandale-on-Hudson: St. Stephen's College, 1933.
Mazure, F. A. J. *Eloge de Montaigne.* Paris: Mame, 1814.
Merleau-Ponty, Maurice. "Lecture de Montaigne," *Les Temps Modernes* (Décembre, 1947).
Merrill, Robert V. *Platonism in French Renaissance Poetry.* New York: New York University Press, 1957.
Mesnard, Pierre. *Essor de la philosophie politique au XVIe siècle.* Paris: Vrin, 1969.
Moët, E. *Des Opinions et des jugements littéraires de Montaigne.* Paris: A. Durand, 1859.
Montaigne, Michel Eyquem de. *The Complete Works of Montaigne.* Translated by Donald Frame. Stanford: Stanford University Press, 1967.
———. *Essais.* 2 vols. Paris: Editions Garnier Frères, 1962.
———. *Essais de Michel Seignevr de Montaigne.* Paris: Abel L'Angelier, 1595.
———. *Journal de voyage.* Paris: Hachette et Cie., 1906.
———. *The Living Thoughts of Montaigne.* Presented by André Gide. New York: Longmans, Green & Co., 1935.
———. *Oeuvres Complètes de Michel de Montaigne.* Vol. I. Etude, commentaires et notes par le Dr. A. Armaingaud. Paris: Louis Conard, 1924.
———. *Thoughts from Montaigne.* Edited by Constance de la Warr. Boston: L. C. Page and Co., 1905.
Morçay, Raoul. "La Renaissance," *Histoire de la littérature française.* Vol. II. Paris: Del Luca, 1967.
Moreau, Pierre. *Montaigne, l'homme et l'œuvre.* Paris: Boivin, 1939.
Murry, John Middleton. *Heaven and Earth.* London: J. Cape, 1938.
———. *Heroes of Thought.* New York: J. Messner, 1938.
Musset, Paul de. "Mademoiselle de Gournay," *Extravagants et originaux du XVIIe siècle.* Paris: Charpentier, 1863.
Nicolaï, Alexandre. "A propos des ascendances de Montaigne," *Revue bleue,* Année 76 (1938).
———. "Les Ascendances de Montaigne," *Revue philomatique de Bordeaux et du Sud-Ouest,* Année 41 (1938).
———. *Les belles amies de Montaigne.* Paris: Editions Dumas, 1950.
Norton, Grace. *The Early Writings of Montaigne.* New York: Macmillan, 1904.
Ovid. *The Art of Love.* Translated by Rolfe Humphries. Bloomington: Indiana University Press, 1969.
Paris, Gaston. *La Littérature française au Moyen Age.* Paris: Hachette, 1913.
Pasquier, Estienne. *Choix de lettres sur la littérature, la langue et la traduction.* Genève: E. Droz, 1956.
Payen, Dr. Jean-François. "Recherches sur Montaigne," *Bulletin du Bibliophile et du Bibliothécaire,* Sér. 15 (1862).
——— et Bastide, J.-B. *Inventaire de la collection Payen, suivi de lettres inédites de Françoise de Lachassagne.* Paris: Léon Téchener, 1878.

SELECTED BIBLIOGRAPHY 101

Pieron, Henri. "Un Précurseur inconnu du féminisme et de la Révolution: Poulain de la Barre," *Revue de Synthèse Historique*, V (Juillet-Décembre, 1902).

Pisan, Christine de. *Oeuvres poétiques de Christine de Pisan*. Edited by Maurice Roy. Paris: Librairie de Firmin Didot et Cie., 1891.

Plattard, Jean. *Etat présent des études sur Montaigne*. Paris: Les Belles Lettres, 1935.

———. *Montaigne et son temps*. Paris: Boivin, 1933.

Plutarch. *Plutarch's Lives*. Vol. I. Translated by Bernadotte Perrin. ("The Loeb Classical Library.") Cambridge: Harvard University Press, 1967.

———. *Plutarch's Moralia*. Vol. VII. Translated by Phillip H. de Lacy. ("The Loeb Classical Library.") Cambridge: Harvard University Press, 1959.

———. *Plutarch's Moralia*. Vol IX. Translated by Edwin L. Minar, Jr. ("The Loeb Classical Library.") Cambridge: Harvard University Press, 1961.

Poulet, Georges. "Montaigne," *Studies in Human Time*. Translated by Elliot Coleman. Baltimore: Johns Hopkins Press, 1956.

Prévost, Jean. *La Vie de Montaigne*. Paris: Gallimard, 1926.

Rabelais, François. *Oeuvres Complètes*. Vol. I. Paris: Garnier Frères, 1962.

Reynier, Gustave. *Le Roman sentimental avant L'Astrée*. Paris: Librairie Armand Collin, 1908.

Richardson, Lula McDovell. *The Forerunners of Feminism in French Literature of the Renaissance*. ("The Johns Hopkins Studies in Romance Literatures and Languages," Vol. XII.) Baltimore: The Johns Hopkins Press, 1929.

Riveline, Maurice. *Montaigne et l'amitié*. Paris: F. Alcan, 1939.

Roth, Cecil. "L'Ascendance juive de Michel de Montaigne," *Revue des Cours et Conférences*, XXXIX (Décembre, 1937-Mars, 1938).

———. "The Montaigne Family Tree," *Personalities and Events in Jewish History*. Philadelphia: The Jewish Publication Society of America, 1953.

Rougemont, Denis de. *Love in the Western World*. Translated by Montgomery Belgion. New York: Pantheon, 1956.

Sainte-Beuve, C. A. *Nouveaux Lundis*. Paris: Calmann-Lévy, n.d.

Saulnier, Verdun L. *Le Dessein de Rabelais*. Paris: Société d'édition d'enseignement supérieur, 1957.

———. *La Littérature française de la Renaissance*. Paris: Presses universitaires de France, 1962.

Schiff, Mario. *La Fille d'alliance de Montaigne, Marie de Gournay*. Paris: Honoré Champion, 1910.

Screech, M. A. "A Further Study of Rabelais' Position in the Querelle des femmes," *François Rabelais. Travaux d'Humanisme et Renaissance*. No. 7. Genève: Librairie E. Droz, 1953.

———. *The Rabelaisian Marriage*. London: Arnold, 1958.

Seltmann, Charles. *Women in Antiquity*. New York: St. Martin's Press, n.d.

Sichel, Edith. *Michel de Montaigne*. London: Constable & Co., Ltd., 1911.

———. *Women and Men of the French Renaissance*. Westminster: Archibald & Co., Ltd., 1902.

Stapfer, Paul. *La Famille et les amis de Montaigne*. Paris: Hachette et Cie., 1896.

———. *Montaigne*. Paris: Hachette et Cie., 1905.

Strowski, Fortunat. *Montaigne*. Paris: Félix Alcan, 1931.

Strowski, Fortunat. *Montaigne: Sa Vie publique et privée.* Paris: La Nouvelle Revue critique, 1938.
Tannenbaum, Samuel. *Michel de Montaigne: A Concise Bibliography.* New York: Samuel Tannenbaum, 1942. (Not critical.)
Telle, Emile V. *L'Œuvre de Marguerite d'Angoulême, reine de Navarre et la querelle des femmes.* Toulouse: Imprimerie Toulasaine, 1937.
Thibaudet, Albert. *Montaigne.* Paris: Gallimard, 1963.
Tilley, Arthur. *The Literature of the French Renaissance.* Cambridge: The University Press, 1904.
———. *Studies in the French Renaissance.* Cambridge: The University Press, 1922.
Tonelli, Luigi. *L'Amore nella poesia et nel pensiero del Rinascimento.* Firenze: G. S. Sansoni, 1933.
Travelyan, Robert Calverley. *Translations from Horace, Juvenal and Montaigne.* Cambridge: The University Press, 1940.
Valency, Maurice. *In Praise of Love: An Introduction to the Love Poetry of the Renaissance.* New York: Macmillan, 1958.
Villey, Pierre L. J. *Les Essais de Michel de Montaigne.* Paris: Nizet, 1946.
———. *Montaigne.* Paris: Les Editions Rieder, 1933.
———. *Montaigne devant la postérité.* Paris: Boivin et Cie., 1935.
———. *Les Sources et l'évolution des Essais de Montaigne.* 2 vols. Paris: Hachette et Cie., 1908.
Virgil. *The Aeneid of Virgil.* Translated by C. Day Lewis. New York: Doubleday Anchor Books, 1953.
Weber, Henri. *La Création poétique au XVIe siècle en France de Maurice Scève à Agrippa d'Aubigné.* Paris: Nizet, 1956.
Weiler, Maurice. *La Pensée de Montaigne.* Paris: Bordas, 1948.
Weinberg, Bernard. *A History of Literary Criticism in the Italian Renaissance.* Chicago: University of Chicago Press, 1963.
Whibley, Charles. *Literary Portraits.* London: A. Constable and Co., Ltd., 1904.
Willis, Irene Cooper. *Montaigne.* New York: Alfred A. Knopf, 1927.

NORTH CAROLINA STUDIES IN THE ROMANCE LANGUAGES AND LITERATURES

I.S.B.N. Prefix 0-8078-

Recent Titles

MOLIÈRE MOCKED. THREE CONTEMPORARY HOSTILE COMEDIES: *Zélinde, Le portrait du peintre, Élomire Hypocondre*, by Frederick Wright Vogler. 1973. (No. 129). *-929-4*.

C.-A. SAINTE-BEUVE. *Chateaubriand et son groupe littéraire sous l'empire*. Index alphabétique et analytique établi par Lorin A. Uffenbeck. 1973. (No. 130). *-930-8*.

THE ORIGINS OF THE BAROQUE CONCEPT OF "PEREGRINATIO," by Juergen Hahn. 1973. (No. 131). *-931-6*.

THE "AUTO SACRAMENTAL" AND THE PARABLE IN SPANISH GOLDEN AGE LITERATURE, by Donald Thaddeus Dietz. 1973. (No. 132). *-932-4*.

FRANCISCO DE OSUNA AND THE SPIRIT OF THE LETTER, by Laura Calvert. 1973. (No. 133). *-933-2*.

ITINERARIO DI AMORE: DIALETTICA DI AMORE E MORTE NELLA VITA NUOVA, by Margherita de Bonfils Templer. 1973. (No. 134). *-934-0*.

L'IMAGINATION POETIQUE CHEZ DU BARTAS: ELEMENTS DE SENSIBILITE BAROQUE DANS LA "CREATION DU MONDE," by Bruno Braunrot. 1973. (No. 135). *-934-0*.

ARTUS DESIRE: PRIEST AND PAMPHLETEER OF THE SIXTEENTH CENTURY, by Frank S. Giese. 1973. (No. 136). *-936-7*.

JARDIN DE NOBLES DONZELLAS, FRAY MARTIN DE CORDOBA, by Harriet Goldberg. 1974. (No. 137). *-937-5*.

MYTHE ET PSYCHOLOGIE CHEZ MARIE DE FRANCE DANS "GUIGEMAR", par Antoinette Knapton. 1975. (No. 142). *-942-1*.

THE LYRIC POEMS OF JEHAN FROISSART: A CRITICAL EDITION, by Rob Roy McGregor, Jr. 1975. (No. 143). *-943-X*.

THE HISPANO-PORTUGUESE CANCIONERO OF THE HISPANIC SOCIETY OF AMERICA, by Arthur Askins. 1974. (No. 144). *-944-8*.

HISTORIA Y BIBLIOGRAFÍA DE LA CRÍTICA SOBRE EL "POEMA DE MÍO CID" (1750-1971), por Miguel Magnotta. 1976. (No. 145). *-945-6*.

LES ENCHANTEMENZ DE BRETAIGNE. AN EXTRACT FROM A THIRTEENTH CENTURY PROSE ROMANCE "LA SUITE DU MERLIN", edited by Patrick C. Smith. 1977. (No. 146). *0-8078-9146-0*.

THE DRAMATIC WORKS OF ÁLVARO CUBILLO DE ARAGÓN, by Shirley B. Whitaker. 1975. (No. 149). *-949-9*.

A CONCORDANCE TO THE "ROMAN DE LA ROSE" OF GUILLAUME DE LORRIS, by Joseph R. Danos. 1976. (No. 156). *0-88438-403-9*.

POETRY AND ANTIPOETRY: A STUDY OF SELECTED ASPECTS OF MAX JACOB'S POETIC STYLE, by Annette Thau. 1976. (No. 158). *-005-X*.

FRANCIS PETRARCH, SIX CENTURIES LATER, by Aldo Scaglione. 1975. (No. 159).

STYLE AND STRUCTURE IN GRACIÁN'S "EL CRITICÓN", by Marcia L. Welles. 1976. (No. 160). *-007-6*.

MOLIERE: TRADITIONS IN CRITICISM, by Laurence Romero. 1974 (Essays, No. 1). *-001-7*.

CHRÉTIEN'S JEWISH GRAIL. A NEW INVESTIGATION OF THE IMAGERY AND SIGNIFICANCE OF CHRÉTIEN DE TROYES'S GRAIL EPISODE BASED UPON MEDIEVAL HEBRAIC SOURCES, by Eugene J. Weinraub. 1976. (Essays, No. 2). *-002-5*.

STUDIES IN TIRSO, I, by Ruth Lee Kennedy. 1974. (Essays, No. 3). *-003-3*.

VOLTAIRE AND THE FRENCH ACADEMY, by Karlis Racevskis. 1975. (Essays, No. 4). *-004-1*.

When ordering please cite the *ISBN Prefix* plus the last four digits for each title.

Send orders to: University of North Carolina Press
Chapel Hill
North Carolina 27514
U. S. A.

NORTH CAROLINA STUDIES IN THE ROMANCE LANGUAGES AND LITERATURES

I.S.B.N. Prefix 0-8078-

Recent Titles

THE NOVELS OF MME RICCOBONI, by Joan Hinde Stewart. 1976. (Essays, No. 8). -008-4.

FIRE AND ICE: THE POETRY OF XAVIER VILLAURRUTIA, by Merlin H. Forster. 1976. (Essays, No. 11). -011-4.

THE THEATER OF ARTHUR ADAMOV, by John J. McCann. 1975. (Essays, No. 13). -013-0.

AN ANATOMY OF POESIS: THE PROSE POEMS OF STÉPHANE MALLARMÉ, by Ursula Franklin. 1976. (Essays, No. 16). -016-5.

LAS MEMORIAS DE GONZALO FERNÁNDEZ DE OVIEDO, Vols. I and II, by Juan Bautista Avalle-Arce. 1974. (Texts, Textual Studies, and Translations, Nos. 1 and 2). -401-2; 402-0.

GIACOMO LEOPARDI: THE WAR OF THE MICE AND THE CRABS, translated, introduced and annotated by Ernesto G. Caserta. 1976. (Texts, Textual Studies, and Translations, No. 4). -404-7.

LUIS VÉLEZ DE GUEVARA: A CRITICAL BIBLIOGRAPHY, by Mary G. Hauer. 1975. (Texts, Textual Studies, and Translations, No. 5). -405-5.

UN TRÍPTICO DEL PERÚ VIRREINAL: "EL VIRREY AMAT, EL MARQUÉS DE SOTO FLORIDO Y LA PERRICHOLI". EL "DRAMA DE DOS PALANGANAS" Y SU CIRCUNSTANCIA, estudio preliminar, reedición y notas por Guillermo Lohmann Villena. 1976. (Texts, Textual Studies, and Translation, No. 15). -415-2.

LOS NARRADORES HISPANOAMERICANOS DE HOY, edited by Juan Bautista Avalle-Arce. 1973. (Symposia, No. 1). -951-0.

ESTUDIOS DE LITERATURA HISPANOAMERICANA EN HONOR A JOSÉ J. ARROM, edited by Andrew P. Debicki and Enrique Pupo-Walker. 1975. (Symposia, No. 2). -952-9.

MEDIEVAL MANUSCRIPTS AND TEXTUAL CRITICISM, edited by Christopher Kleinhenz. 1976. (Symposia, No. 4). -954-5.

SAMUEL BECKETT. THE ART OF RHETORIC, edited by Edouard Morot-Sir, Howard Harper, and Dougald McMillan III. 1976. (Symposia, No. 5). -955-3.

DELIE. CONCORDANCE, by Jerry Nash. 1976. 2 Volumes. (No. 174).

FIGURES OF REPETITION IN THE OLD PROVENÇAL LYRIC: A STUDY IN THE STYLE OF THE TROUBADOURS, by Nathaniel B. Smith. 1976. (No. 176). 0-8078-9176-2.

A CRITICAL EDITION OF LE REGIME TRESUTILE ET TRESPROUFITABLE POUR CONSERVER ET GARDER LA SANTE DU CORPS HUMAIN, by Patricia Willett Cummins. 1977. (No. 177).

THE DRAMA OF SELF IN GUILLAUME APOLLINAIRE'S "ALCOOLS", by Richard Howard Stamelman. 1976. (No. 178). 0-8078-9178-9.

A CRITICAL EDITION OF "LA PASSION NOSTRE SEIGNEUR" FROM MANUSCRIPT 1131 FROM THE BIBLIOTHEQUE SAINTE-GENEVIEVE, PARIS, by Edward J. Gallagher. 1976. (No. 179). 0-8078-9179-7.

A QUANTITATIVE AND COMPARATIVE STUDY OF THE VOCALISM OF THE LATIN INSCRIPTIONS OF NORTH AFRICA, BRITAIN, DALMATIA, AND THE BALKANS, by Stephen William Omeltchenko. 1977. (No. 180). 0-8078-9180-0.

OCTAVIEN DE SAINT-GELAIS "LE SEJOUR D'HONNEUR", edited by Joseph A. James. 1977. (No. 181). 0-8078-9181-9.

THE LIFE AND WORKS OF LUIS CARLOS LÓPEZ, by Martha S. Bazik. 1977. (No. 183). 0-8078-9183-5.

When ordering please cite the *ISBN Prefix* plus the last four digits for each title.

Send orders to: University of North Carolina Press
Chapel Hill
North Carolina 27514
U. S. A.

The Department of Romance Studies Digital Arts and Collaboration Lab at the University of North Carolina at Chapel Hill is proud to support the digitization of the North Carolina Studies in the Romance Languages and Literatures series.

www.ingramcontent.com/pod-product-compliance
Lightning Source LLC
Chambersburg PA
CBHW020421230426
43663CB00007BA/1259